Preventing Accidents and Illness at work

HEALTH &
SAFETY IN
PRACTICE

Preventing Accidents and Illness at work

How to create a Health and Safety Culture

Steve Morris and
Graham Willcocks

London · Hong Kong · Johannesburg · Melbourne
Singapore · Washington DC

PITMAN PUBLISHING
128 Long Acre, London WC2E 9AN
Tel: +44 (0) 171 447 2000
Fax: +44 (0) 171 240 5771

A Division of Pearson Professional Limited

First published in Great Britain, 1996

© Pearson Professional Limited 1996

British Library Cataloguing in Publication Data
A CIP catalogue record for this book can be obtained from the British Library.

ISBN 0 273 61687 0

10 9 8 7 6 5 4 3 2 1

Typeset by Northern Phototypesetting Co Ltd., Bolton
Printed and bound in Great Britain by Bell & Bain Ltd., Glasgow

The Publishers' policy is to use paper manufactured from sustainable forests

About the authors

Steve Morris, director of the Burton Morris Consultancy, is an experienced writer of books, articles and action guides on management. He has recently completed several projects for companies including: The Health & Safety Executive, The National Consumer Council and The National Health Service Management Executive. He has also worked for private sector companies such as Ind Coope, The Institute of Management and Forte Posthouse, developing materials on leadership and is consultant for the Institute of Personnel and Development, the University of London and the University of the West Indies.

Graham Willcocks is a director of Wesley House Consultancy. He is a writer, trainer and process consultant. He has had wide management experience in both the private and public sectors, developing programmes on health & safety, leadership, teams, change, customer care and strategic marketing within a wide range of organisations. He is also a fellow of the Institute of Personnel Development.

Contents

Preface   ix
This is not a boring book!   ix
What's different in this book?   x
Using this book   xi

1 Why health and safety matters   1
Health and safety: everybody's issue   3
Health and safety responsibility   5
Costs and benefits of a positive approach to health
     and safety   6
The costs of safety   14
A quality approach and the positive benefits   18
Health and safety and management thinking   21

2 Towards a healthy and safe organisation   29
What are we talking about?   30
Prevention   34
The costs of not getting health and safety right   38
The costs of a positive health and safety approach   45
Some basic health and safety principles   47
Attitude problems and the basic principles   53
Planning some action   54

3 Where are we, and where are we going?   57
Auditing   58
Health and safety and continuous improvement   60
Three areas in an organisation safety audit   62
Building the health and safety specification   73
Carrying out the audit   82
Planning some action   86

4 Playing your part in health and safety   89
Health and safety culture and people   90

Senior managers   91
Middle managers   101
Supervisors and other front line managers   105
Front line staff   108
Planning some action   109

5 Assessing the risks   113
There's always the risk …   114
The risk assessment process   114
A systematic approach to risk assessment   118
The bridge from risk assessment to health and
   safety culture   129

6 Raising the health and safety profile   135
Telling the truth   136
What are your information systems like at the moment?   137
Thinking through information flows   138
Developing a six point action plan   142
Making the plan work   150
Some ideas for raising the profile   151
Using training   159
Raising the profile face to face   160
The training events   162

7 Making it work for you   165
Techniques for making progress   167
Training for a safer workplace   175
The health and safety action plan   182
Conclusion   190

Index   191

Preface

THIS IS NOT A BORING BOOK!

Health and safety is about sticking to the rules and it's boring. Well, that's often its image. People think of it as being about scaffolding and the right number of WCs, or regulations that stop you doing things instead of helping you get things done, and bureaucratic inspectors who are out to get you if they can.

Look at it like this, of course it's boring. But this is a historical perspective that has developed over time and hasn't been brought up to date. It simply isn't a view that helps organisations succeed in today's business world. When children went up chimneys and the UK was a mass of dark satanic mills, the emphasis had to be on forcing changes through legislation and punishment. But that's largely been done, and while there is always a need to update and modernise regulations to reflect technological and social change, the laws are in place. The issue now is about the values and beliefs, the organisational culture that has to be established now that things have changed and are changing.

So, the first message is that health and safety simply isn't boring any longer – or if it is then there's a huge problem to be solved, because health and safety is a central and major factor in organisational success. It sits alongside quality, customer care, and teamwork as an issue that can make or break businesses in today's competitive climate.

You may find all this hard to swallow, because the traditional view of health and safety is of a series of hurdles that you have to clear to stay on the right side of the law. This view has been fostered by the way the whole area has been tackled by government, inspectors, managers and employees, and it has turned an exciting and vibrant business issue into a negative experience. You have to do it, rather than you want to do it, and whenever that is the case, human beings dig their heels in and resist.

Mind you, the legal pressure is there, and you can't ignore it. All we're saying is that it's an opportunity missed if you throw the baby out with the bath water. Don't reject or resist positive moves on health and safety, just because there is an element of compulsion somewhere in the background. The aim of this book is to prove that the most persuasive and powerful reasons for taking health and safety measures are the ones you define for yourself, and not the ones that are imposed from outside. So please, to get the real benefit from this book, suspend any negative and cynical views you have now, and see where the book takes you.

WHAT'S DIFFERENT IN THIS BOOK?

This book turns the traditional view of health and safety on its head and puts it in its right context as a central business issue at the end of the twentieth century. Health and safety is about people, problem-solving, and respect for others and yourself. It's also about profits, and you will see how simple it is to work out the really massive costs of not taking it seriously. It's about business success, teamwork, communication and everyone – from top managers to front line workers – working together to enhance the reputation and achievements of the organisation.

One of the things that's different about this book is that it doesn't promise you quick fixes. We know there are no magic answers. Any problem that has become as deep-rooted as this one is not going to be solved overnight. It's a long hard slog to influence people's perceptions, and to win over their hearts and minds. And that's what you have to do, because you probably know from experience that telling someone to conform to the legal requirements – and threatening them if they don't – is more often than not a waste of time. It leads to confrontation, an 'us and them' attitude, and a culture that sets people apart from each other. And it doesn't get the required results, either.

One reason that staff in organisations do not do what their managers tell them with regard to health and safety is simple and potentially embarrassing. It is that managers are often hypocritical. They say that something is top priority, issue directives and procedures that spell out how people have to behave, then behave in a way that is diametrically opposed to what they require of others. Or, when the pressure is on, they tell people to forget the good stuff they were preaching last week, and cut corners to get this job finished. This undermines every principle of good practice, and makes health and safety seem like an umbrella that you use when the sun's shining, and put away when the rain starts.

So, effective health and safety is a cultural issue, about people's behaviour, values, beliefs and priorities. And it isn't easy at the start – although it does become easier.

USING THE BOOK

This book sets out to help you do three things to get the ball rolling:

- understand the real issues in health and safety, the aspects that demonstrate what it is and show that it is not anything like you thought it was

- take ownership of the values, knowledge and attitudes that are covered, and feel powerful enough to start trying to get them across to others – to be a sort of advocate

- find techniques and approaches that will let you start making a real difference to people's behaviour, and so to the culture of your organisation.

You will notice that this last point says that the techniques help you influence behaviour and culture. That's because you have to work on the values, beliefs and attitudes of people at all levels, if you are really going to make any difference.

Cultural change is a slow and difficult process. It never happens because someone says it will – it happens over time, as people see different behavioural trends emerging and more respectful ways of doing things, until they come to accept that this is the way this organisation really works. People need evidence if they are going to believe you and take health and safety seriously.

So, you need evidence too. Nobody expects you to get excited or switched on to health and safety just because a couple of guys say it's a great idea. You need and deserve evidence and information – and that's what this book is really all about.

One final thought; how likely is it that your attitudes on health and safety can be changed? Ours were. A couple of years ago, we thought health and safety was boring, and we nearly turned down a consultancy because we work on change issues, teamwork, leadership and human topics like that ... not on stuff that centres on strict procedures and wearing protective gloves. As we worked through the consultancy, the light started to dawn and we recognised clearly the crucial importance of health and safety to the organisation and its business. We were converted then, and have not been disabused of our beliefs since.

So, we hope you find this book entertaining, enlightening and informative ... and above all, useful and relevant to your own situation.

Why health and safety matters

Two colleagues were having a drink at the end of a day's managing.

'I'm convinced we could do better at health and safety.'

'We do all right now. We spend a lot on guards, rails and all the bits and pieces that we have to by law.'

'Yes, but I feel we don't work together on it as a team across the firm. I think we just stand by and let things go wrong in other departments – even when we can see there's going to be a problem.'

'But that's how managers work! I manage my bit of the firm and you manage yours. Nobody tells me I'm wrong! Apart from anything else, if a real problem blows up I don't need anyone else saying that they warned me in advance, thank you very much. That would put me in real trouble. I issue the instructions to the workers, and if they ignore them it's their look-out.'

'But surely, if someone working for you could help you stop an accident and save you having to explain why it had happened, wouldn't that be useful?'

I'm the boss. I don't need bloody workers telling me how to do my job. It's how the firm has run for years – everyone left to fight it out for themselves. Nobody ever listened to me when I was on the shop floor, and I suggested ways of making it safer – and if it was good enough for me it's good enough for them.'

'Well, I disagree. Today my chief clerk did something really simple and saved me a lot of embarrassment – and someone a bad injury. It was only a small split in the carpet, but she kept tripping over it so she took the initiative and got maintenance to repair it.'

'She got maintenance in? Don't they need your authorisation?'

'In the past, yes, but last week at the staff briefing I asked them to take more responsibility. I delegated the authority to deal with simple problems, and I told Dave in maintenance what I'd done, so he would get on with it without referring back to me all the time.'

'Bloody anarchy, if you ask me. Oh – oops – you all right? Y'know, I could see you were going to slip on that wet patch. Do you want a hanky for the blood?'

One of the masters of Total Quality Management, W Edwards Deming, is quoted as saying:

You do not have to do this. Survival is not compulsory.

In other words, life is a series of free choices and nobody can make you do anything if you're determined not to. So, you are entirely at liberty to do as little as possible about health and safety, hope for the best and say that's your considered choice – to maintain that you're the one with the authority to make decisions, and this is your decision.

But the trouble with this approach to health and safety is two-fold:

● there are laws and regulations that mean you have to comply, or you and your organisation can end up in real legal trouble

● it is a flawed – and essentially stupid – way of running any business. Potentially it damages other people, it damages the organisation's reputation, profits and progress, and it damages you as a human being. So it's stupid, because you have the chance to limit the damage and the only thing stopping you … is you.

This book has been written to explain why this is a flawed approach, and how you can develop a more positive approach that will bring you and your organisation more success, fewer problems and a greater sense of team spirit. You probably wouldn't have bought the book in the first place unless you wanted to develop a positive health and safety culture, but just in case someone else bought it for you anonymously and left it on your desk … stick with it and read on. You'll find it makes sense and, to start us off, we're going to look at some logical arguments in favour of a positive approach to health and safety. After all, even the most sceptical individuals tend to pay closer attention and get more involved as they can recognise the prospects of real benefits for themselves and their organisation – and this question of involvement sits right at the heart of the issue.

Managers commonly believe they have dealt with the health and safety issue by giving it all to someone else to look after and then assuming it's gone away. Some organisations employ or designate someone as the health and safety manager, and believe that by doing this and nothing else, everything is covered. There's no denying that having a specialist in the post can generally make a real contribution to the culture, but that is not the same as shrugging off responsibility yourself and leaving it to someone else. Let's look at why abdication is the wrong tactic.

HEALTH AND SAFETY: EVERYBODY'S ISSUE

Have you ever worked (or do you work) in an organisation where every specialist responsibility is handled by someone employed specifically to cope with the issues it covers? You know the sort of thing – a quality manager is responsible for all the quality, a personnel manager looks after all the recruitment and performance management activities, and a health and safety manager is there to look after all the health and safety.

If you have, you'll recognise the real dangers of this approach, especially when the other managers and employees are heard to say:

'You'd better speak to X about that – quality is her business.'

'You're still not doing well enough. I'm reporting you to personnel so they can consider disciplinary action.'

'The accident's down to the health and safety manager, isn't it?'

Sorry ... the expert is not in

A traditional role of the Careers Service is helping young people find appropriate employment and further education, among other key tasks. In the late 1980s in one County Careers Service, the management identified specific groups of young people in need of extra attention. The groups included ethnic minorities, more able students, people with disabilities, young offenders and long-term unemployed.

The management worked hard to raise the resources needed to handle the needs of these groups, and set up teams of three or four Careers Officers for each group, spread around the county.

The result was that if a young black person, someone in a wheelchair, or an individual with exceptionally good 'A' level grades seeking a university place called into an office and the specialist was out, they were likely to be sent away again because 'their' Careers Officer had to see them.

▶

▶

Eventually, the inevitable happened. A hearing-impaired black girl, who had left school, been unemployed for a year and occupied her time studying at home with the aim of retaking 'A' levels, had got excellent grades and the chance of an Oxbridge place.

The specialist officers couldn't work out who should see her, so they had to hold a group meeting – one client and three officers. Soon after that the Service learned from the situation and developed a generic approach, where every Careers Officer saw people. (People was the technical term used.) They cut the number of specialist officers down to one per special group and changed their role to a sort of 'internal consultant', to whom colleagues referred people only if there was a real need for technical or specialist help.

In other words, in the light of experience this particular Careers Service decided that the best approach was for everyone to deal with people, with the option of using experts as consultants whenever things got really tough or technical. The rationale was that the people – the young clients – were the real reason the Service and the jobs existed, and the way the service was structured had to reflect that.

In all organisations, issues like quality, performance management and health and safety are too important to be given away to others by senior and line managers. Take a couple of situations that could involve a personnel manager.

● Someone working for you turns up late every day. Would you really want to leave it to the personnel manager to tell a member of your team that their lateness caused a problem? If you do, your authority is undermined immediately, you give away a large chunk of the status and management role that you have worked hard to achieve, and you lose your grip on issues that are within your own span of control.

● Or, what if you want to replace an employee who is leaving. Passing over recruitment and selection wholesale to someone in personnel would potentially leave you out of the picture, or with only a small part to play. You might get someone you wouldn't have chosen, or the personnel manager might not understand the intricacies of the role you want filled. The bottom line is you would have no-one to blame but yourself. Mind you, you would probably blame personnel as it was their choice – but you'd be wrong because you set that situation up, by default. You can't have it both ways.

Authority, responsibility and accountability go hand in hand. Management in today's organisations is about a more holistic approach, where every manager plays a significant part in what may have been traditionally specialist and separate functions like personnel management. Teams, flatter management structures, cross-functional communication, breaking down barriers and opening up the organisation – these are all current topics you'll read about in any number of journals and books, reflecting the way effective management thinking goes. So passing the buck to someone else isn't an option.

Quality is another issue we mentioned. Look back a few years and quality may have been managed by a few people in white coats (either real or metaphorical) whose job was to spot and weed out the mistakes other people made. Modern quality management has left that sort of approach behind, on the basis that unless everyone looks after the quality of the products and services they contribute to the overall output, 99% of the staff don't take it seriously.

HEALTH AND SAFETY RESPONSIBILITY

The purpose of a positive health and safety culture is to have people working together, identifying formally and informally areas and practices that could cause harm to themselves or others, and co-operating to prevent it happening. That's all there is to it, and you might say that that's obvious – it's what the law says has to happen anyway. And you'd be right – it is what the law says.

The critical perspective

All the issues you've just read about for personnel and quality apply as much, if not more, to health and safety. It isn't one person's responsibility and you can't make any real improvements unless everyone is in there, doing their bit and seeing health and safety as their own issue. So what does the law say? To find out in detail, get a copy of the relevant legislation and check it for yourself, but in essence the Health and Safety at Work Act 1974 says the following about who is responsible for what:

- employers have overall responsibility for health and safety and a duty towards employees, visitors – and anyone else who could be affected by what individuals and the firm do or make

● employees must be careful not to endanger the health and safety of their colleagues or anyone else who could be affected.

Now, you might say that there's nothing here that you didn't know. It's obviously everyone's responsibility. Everyone at work has to make sure they don't take actions that jeopardise the health and safety of themselves, others at work, or anyone else who might be affected by what they do. So what's new?

It's not so much what's new as what's the new perspective. We'd like to turn this round and put a different slant on it. A positive health and safety culture means more than not doing dangerous things, which is a relatively passive approach. It means doing things to remove or reduce danger, by taking active and positive steps to improve the chances of a safe and healthy environment for everyone.

This different perspective might seem like a small shift, but think about it. Instead of just sticking to the rules and doing things by the book – which no-one denies is crucial to good health and safety – we're saying that everybody's focus should be on looking for improvements, and making them. So nothing detrimental should be done – but in addition, the aim should be to start and maintain a perpetual quest by all employees for a healthier and safer workplace.

This aim is the heart of this book, and achieving it isn't easy. You need to stop everyone believing that health and safety is someone else's problem, and get them to start believing it's their responsibility.

To reach this point you need to help everyone convince themselves that health and safety really does matter to them. This requires you to do more than simply tell them that that's what the law says. It means getting them to own the philosophy and see for themselves why they need to be committed to a positive health and safety approach.

COSTS AND BENEFITS OF A POSITIVE APPROACH TO HEALTH AND SAFETY

If you're running any sort of organisation – or any part of one – you know that there are always costs and benefits to be considered in any decision. Even in the home, there is a balance between the benefits of a new kitchen, car or carpet, and the costs. You ask yourself what each side of the equation looks like, so you can work out where the balance comes down, and you make your decision on the basis of sensible analysis.

In any analysis of this sort there are masses of things to consider and they tend to fall into two categories – financial and 'other'. Say you are thinking about a new coupé car, now the children have left home. The financial balance is between its price and any extra running and insurance costs on the one hand, and, on the other hand, any savings on fuel economy, servicing and repairs. You also need to think about what else you could do with the money you plan to spend on buying the new model, and so on.

The non-financial costs include the loss of flexibility in moving from a four to a two door model, the amount of luggage space et cetera. The non-financial benefits include the image you project, the feeling you get and the status you feel it gives you.

Overall, nobody makes any decision unless the benefits outweigh the costs – even if it doesn't look that way to an outsider. So, maybe you feel that a friend incurs unnecessary financial costs when they change their car ... but to them the increased status is worth every penny, and more.

In health and safety the same equation applies. All the advertising in the world and all the threats of legal sanctions do not work unless the individual concerned can see what's in it for them. This has been the case for years, and the proof turns up in organisations that simply don't take health and safety seriously. People get ill, have accidents and near misses, and put themselves at risk every day, but the people involved are simply not convinced that the benefits of taking it seriously outweigh the costs.

Who are these people?

They're everybody. They're board members and senior managers who decide how the organisation works and what its priorities are. They're middle and junior managers who don't put health and safety high enough on their own agenda, preferring to do just enough or nearly enough to get through a possible inspection. And they're the employees who have heard all the words, read all the posters, and still ignore what they have been told.

What they all have in common is that the culture they work in gives everyone the same message – health and safety is not genuinely a high priority around here.

Top managers

It really has to start here, at the top. If top managers truly believe that health and safety is crucial to a successful business and not merely a nuisance, other people will take it seriously. You'll see quite a lot of evidence for this in Chapter 6, but for now think about real situations where you work.

Think about an occasion when top managers started some sort of initiative – customer care maybe, or a drive for greater productivity. But senior managers themselves didn't act as role models, didn't do themselves what they were telling everyone else they had to do, so it didn't work. This top-down commitment is crucially important to any culture change, whether it's introducing Total Quality Management, developing more open communications or aiming to improve time-keeping. If it isn't there, people always end up saying, 'if it's good enough for us, it has to be good enough for them'.

This doesn't mean that you can't make any progress without top managers driving the process, but having them take the lead makes life so much easier. If they aren't fully committed you have to start small, maybe limiting action to your own area of responsibility, and influencing culture from the inside. Eventually it will trickle upwards, when top people see the benefits. However, it has to be said again clearly, a good deal of the effort you are prepared to spend on devel-oping a positive health and safety culture is best invested in convin-cing senior management, if they're not already convinced; because of their massive influence on the organisation's culture.

Middle managers

This group will be much easier to win over if the top managers set the tone properly and demonstrate their own commitment to the cause. The reasons that top managers take it seriously don't matter – what matters is that they start to insist that health and safety is a serious business issue, and that everyone must work towards a more positive approach. Their more junior colleagues will then conform to this lead.

Whichever way you cut it, the eventual responsibility rests firmly on the shoulders of managers – all managers from the top down. It's their role to work at sorting this out, because it's managers who set the tone and lead the development of the organisation's culture. Your role is to influence and develop their thinking and values, so they take over ownership of the issues.

Other staff

The cascading approach fits here, too. If the organisation operates in a way that demonstrates its disapproval of poor health and safety practice, people will come round and adopt the culture. Front line employees adopt the attitudes and practices of managers. If the entire organisation demonstrates regularly and clearly that the required standards of behaviour are based on good practice, then those good practices start to take hold.

There are always exceptions to this, of course, but they are just as cultural as the other issues. For instance, many men are macho, especially when they work in male-dominated environments. They don't like to be seen as wimps and, unfortunately, wearing protective clothing or rubbing in barrier cream is not always thought to be manly on, say, a building site where the culture reeks of testosterone. This peer culture is just as influential in developing good and bad practices, and later in the book we'll explore ways of tackling this part of the problem.

But for now, let's work on the most critical aspect – the influence senior managers have on culture, and the effect the culture has on the chances of identifying and making constructive improvements and changes.

Culture and culture change

Culture is an important aspect of this book, so let's establish a working definition and have a look at your organisation's culture. The definition we'll use is a simple one. It's:

> *The way we do things round here.*

In other words, there are normal behaviours that mark out how an organisation operates, and they affect every single part of it. So, if managers normally behave in an autocratic and directive way, that's how the organisation will work. If management actions demonstrate that profits come before people, that's the value system at work, and how the whole place feels to work in. That's how all issues get looked at and it becomes the culture, the normal set of behaviours. Every new decision that has to be taken is approached in the same way, so it fits in with the normal behaviour in the organisation.

If the culture is one where managers don't really encourage every-one to play an active part in identifying and implementing improve-ments for the organisation, it doesn't matter what they say. Similarly, where departments are at war rather than on the same side, there will be immense difficulties in implementing improvements and changes to health and safety.

The following descriptions relate specifically to culture in a context of change. Even if you have managed to get across that the benefits of a different health and safety perspective outweigh the costs, it isn't always as easy as it could be to get the change into place. The way the whole organisation deals with innovation, change and improvement is going to be a major factor in the battle to move forward.

Have a look at the following four different approaches to culture. Think about your organisation and pick the description that most clearly matches it. If you work somewhere where the approach is a mixture of more than one type, note down which aspects of the descriptions remind you of your own situation.

Animal farm

The way organisations respond or react to change can be seen as descrip-tions of different animals. Is yours ...

An ostrich
Change hits the organisation where it hurts. No planning or preparation has been done as the stance taken is that, 'if we bury our heads in the sand it will all go away'. The effect of burying one's head is to expose other parts of the corporate anatomy. Communications are poor and people look out for themselves, seeing the public as a passive mass about whose needs they know best. Often it is characterised by organisations with wonderfully worded mission and value statements and policies – but without the hard corporate objectives, strategies and plans to deliver them. Increasingly, these organisations deny reality, and move towards a continuous justification of their own position in the face of the facts and the evidence. When things go wrong, a lot of time and effort is spent explaining why the organisation is right and the complainer wrong.

A headless chicken
There is surprise that what has been on the cards for some time has really happened. There has been no corporate planning for contingencies and suddenly it is clear that the change is coming on Monday. Everyone assumes it is someone else's problem and blames others for having done nothing about it. Separate parts of the organisation panic and run round in small circles, with no interdepartmental co–ordination. Occasionally the impact is on one department only, and the others breathe a sigh of relief and may even gloat, just a little. Expertise is not shared and this increases the interdepartmental fortress mentality. In a crisis, the same few entrepreneurial people seem to come to the rescue, despite the system and the organisation. Most of the time the organisation struggles through, but stress levels are high and morale low.

A spider
The spider waits for something to hit its web – which is sensitive to external impact – and delivers a rapid response. It does not go out and explore, it just sits there waiting for something to happen. It is reactive, but has planned its reaction. Because the impact is from outside, it mirrors organisations that monitor the external political, economic, social and technological environment and sets up project teams to respond to whatever events occur or are about to occur. It is effective as a rapid response force, but tends to sit there without any growth or action until there is something to respond to. Managers in organisations that operate in this way tend to fight fires instead of preventing them.

A sheepdog
A good sheepdog is always prepared to move its flock – its organisation – forward. As long as it does not change situations for the sake of it, it is an effective and active planner. Top management watches the environment, and reacts to any message and clue as to where to go next, but it is always thinking ahead, anticipating movement and planning moves to achieve the best possible outcome with the least trauma. All managers are encouraged to set objectives and identify where they are now, where they ought to be and how to get there – actively managing change. While change for its own sake increases waste and stress, effective planning and management of change reduces both waste and stress.

Reproduced with permission of Wesley House Consultants ©

If yours is anything other than a sheepdog, our sympathies are with you – but nobody ever said that making progress was easy, and the fact that it's hard is no reason not to try. It simply means you need to do that bit more analysis and planning, to strengthen the argument and make it one that fits the culture and supports the value system. It would be pointless and daft to expect you – or anyone else – to change the way managers behave unless they can see that the benefits to them outweigh the costs. So, if you focus on top managers, you know they need evidence to show that there is a clear pay-off for the organisation, its shareholders, and themselves.

Here's one very powerful message, that can work in organisations where there is an 'us and them' attitude. The message is:

> *Either everybody wins, or everybody loses.*

Winners and losers

In a health and safety failure, there are no winners. An accident has financial and non-financial costs for the organisation and the individual involved. On the other hand, a lack of problems and an excellent record in health and safety is to everyone's advantage.

In organisations where management believes that anything the employees want must be bad for profits, this basic message has to be conveyed clearly, powerfully and consistently. If anyone argues, ask them who wins if staff are off sick because of work-related illness or accident. We'll examine the facts behind this message shortly, but before we go on to the hard evidence, here's a tip on how to structure the case and make it one that will find a more willing audience, when the time comes.

The 'so what' approach to selling health and safety

Any really successful sales person will tell you that people buy benefits, not features. They buy what the product or service will do for them, not the technical features that turn on the experts.

In a small survey about why people bought a fax for use at home:

- 32% said their work extended from their normal workplace or office into the home and they needed access to a fax for business
- 17% said they used it to communicate with friends who had a fax
- 44% said they worked at home as self-employed people
- 7% loved gadgets and wanted to own whatever was new.

Nobody said they bought their fax because it worked at a modem speed of 9600 bps, or even because it held a paper roll 30 metres long. If the sales person had said that, the buyer would probably have said, 'So what?'

Then the benefits would have emerged. The answers to the question, 'so what', might have gone like this.

'Well, 9600 bps is jargon, that means it's fast at sending and receiving messages, so it saves you time and it cuts your telephone bill.'

'Well, having a paper roll that long means you have fewer problems – you don't need to replace it so often and you run out of paper in the middle of a fax far less frequently.'

Spot the benefits – the reduced phone bills, the shorter times and the fewer problems? It is very likely that nobody has ever before made a case out to you for a positive attitude to health and safety as a real business asset, stressing the benefits. Instead, the chances are that the legal and regulatory approach – you must do this or you are breaking the law – has been tried. The same thing is true up and down all organisations, with a few very enlightened exceptions.

1

Personal profile

My job in the University meant I looked after health and safety in the department. The way it worked was that my job description set out clear targets, and because my predecessor had done virtually nothing about it, anything over that was an improvement. The powers that be were under pressure to be seen to conform to the law, so they decided that I should identify at least six improvements in health and safety in the first year. The intention was to increase the target each year, but they apparently forgot about that, and as long as I got my six each year, I got good results at my annual appraisal.

It didn't take me long to realise there were lots more than six improvements, staring me in the face. But I had to write quite detailed reports on the areas I identified and how I tackled them. So I used to keep quiet about anything too complex or over the bare minimum of six, and select areas that didn't take up too much time. They set the targets – I met them. I did what they required, and it was an absolutely ridiculous charade. It made only the most trivial difference to the real situation, but we played the numbers game and I stuck to the rules.

Scottish University Lecturer

Maybe if someone had set about getting the real message across, and demonstrated powerfully and clearly that health and safety is about people's welfare, friends' health and colleagues' freedom from pain and injury, it might have made a difference. But the benefits were never clarified – just the potential personal costs for the individual lecturer, if she failed to come up with the right numbers and the appropriate forms.

The culture set from the top was one where doing enough to get by was the required behaviour, so that's what happened. The real benefits were never examined, let alone discussed and shared as common issues.

Think about it ...

What are the costs and benefits of health and safety management, as you and your organisation see them at the moment?

In many cases, the equation that forms the answer is so basic it seems logical. The potential costs are a fine from an inspector, and the actual costs are the bare minimum needed. The benefits of doing anything at all are minimal – that you can survive an inspection, and you can produce all the right bits of paper if someone asks. The benefits of doing as little as possible are that it doesn't interfere with the real work.

Let's start by challenging this equation.

THE COSTS OF SAFETY

Chapter 2 is where we explore costs and their implications in detail, but here the focus is on the underlying management principles of comparing costs with investment.

Investment or expense

Some organisations really don't believe that spending on health and safety is an investment. Anything spent is a dead cost, because they don't have a problem and the spend brings no return. This is prevalent in organisations where doing little or nothing hasn't caused them any real problems in the past. They have not had an accident, caused any industrial illnesses or failed an inspection. So costs involved in health and safety management are seen as an expense and not an investment.

The bottom line is that nothing has gone wrong so far, so the idea of any problems arising is answered with an, 'it always happens to someone else, it won't happen to me' approach. If someone really believes this, then any expenditure on health and safety is, in their eyes, a drain on resources. But is this really a sophisticated and credible management philosophy? Is blind faith, a lack of forecasting and planning, and a refusal to examine the evidence, the mark of an effective manager in the late twentieth century? Is it the way the rest of the organisation's policies and strategies are devised? No, not really.

This is a real problem area, when you're trying to convince people that taking health and safety seriously is cheaper financially in the long run than doing nothing. But it is an issue where there are many parallels that can bring the truth home. Here are a few, expressed as questions you might like to answer yourself, and use later in your efforts to get the point across to others.

Parallels with costs and benefits of health and safety

- Because you spend money on home insurance, would you rather that someone did break into your house and steal your belongings, so that you get value for money?

- After twenty years of driving without an accident, how sorry are you that you never had a costly accident?

- Why do you spend money servicing the car?

- What happens to your motor insurance premiums if you have an accident?

- What sort of maintenance schedules are there for equipment at work? Why are these schedules introduced?

The answers to questions like these are fairly straightforward, for most people. Yes – insurance is a cost and it can be a pain to pay it every year. But would you really want to cut off your nose to spite your face, and get your money's worth through a burglary or a car accident. And would you be prepared to become a bad risk and pay increased premiums every year after that?

Similarly, you spend money servicing the car and maintaining equipment because it stops it going wrong. It's an investment, based on the premise that prevention is better than cure. These and similar examples are accepted as simple common sense, just as readily as people accept that health and safety is different. But it isn't different – it's a direct parallel.

The parallel is a simple one. It is that spending time and money on positive steps to keep the workplace healthy and safe saves much more in the long run than it costs immediately. Maybe there is no argument against someone who says they have managed to get away with it for twenty years, except to say that it's really no way to run a business. Luck is not a skill mentioned in any standard management textbook. Would you invest money in a firm that said proudly in its company report that:

> *In the coming year as in past years, we are relying on good luck to find new customers and ensure that the plant stays open. We aim to stay in profit by buying several lottery tickets each week.*

Accidents are insured anyway

One argument that comes up is that everything is insured anyway, so paying that premium covers virtually every eventuality. But is it all insured? HSE say that, compared with insured losses, uninsured losses from poor health and safety cost organisations at least six times as much as they pay in insurance premiums. At the top end of the range it can reach almost thirty times as much, so for the sake of argument let's assume an average of about fifteen times the amount of premiums. This means that, for every £1,000 your organisation pays in insurance premiums it ought to bank on paying out a further £15,000 to cover what isn't insured. This sort of loss has sent many a company down.

In any event, think about insurance as a business and take just one issue – that of increased premiums as a cost of an accident. Accept the premise that insurance companies need to make profits, just as much as any other concern, and then imagine what level of premiums they need to collect and what sort of loading they apply to poor risk companies, in order to cover the 1990 level of claims for injury and ill health under employers' liability. Bear in mind that they have to pay the claims, and make enough profit to run their businesses and pay dividends to shareholders. The payout in 1990, by the way, was over £300 million – and it shows every sign of continuing to rise as it has for several years past.

A few more facts

If you feel reassured because all real accidents happen in factories and you work in a nice, clean office or shop ... then don't. Accidents happen anywhere and it isn't the big dramatic ones that cause most problems.

Test your knowledge

Let's take a year at random – 1992. For every one person in the HSE statistics for that year who was injured or killed by moving machinery, how many do you think were:

a) hurt by slips, falls and trips at the level they were working at

c) injured while carrying, handling or lifting something?

1

The answers are that, compared with those injured by machines, about three and a half times as many people slipped, fell or tripped and were off work for significant periods as a result. Well over six times as many – almost 53,000 – had to stay off work because of injuries while lifting, handling or carrying something. So it isn't the headline-grabbing incidents that do the damage. It's the everyday things that can – and do – go wrong anywhere.

Again in the 1992 HSE figures, over 29 million working days (and that's the reported ones) were lost through injury. The aim of positive health and safety management is to make sure your organisation doesn't contribute to these horrendous statistics. In this area, no news really is good news.

This has to be managed. It does not happen on its own – well, not forever, anyway. Organisations may be lucky for a time, even a long time, but in the end something will happen that leads everyone to wish they had planned and implemented systems, procedures and practices that prevented or reduced the risk of an accident or incident.

A QUALITY APPROACH AND THE POSITIVE BENEFITS

There are huge benefits to be gained from a positive health and safety culture and an active, creative approach. Let's draw another parallel and look again at a point you have seen a couple of times; compare the characteristics of a constructive approach to quality management with what is appropriate in health and safety.

Old fashioned quality management

Quality management traditionally worked on the basis that a set level of error and failure was expected and built into the system. So, a manufacturer might have said that 96% of all products would be perfect by the time they reached the end of the production line. This obviously meant that 4% was going to be wrong, and everyone worked on that assumption. Put simply, the assumption was that 96% was good enough. To find the 4% that was wrong, special inspectors were put on the line to weed out the failures and scrap them, so that only perfect products got through to customers.

There were costs involved in employing and resourcing quality inspectors and controllers – whose only role was to find the planned mistakes. When they did, the costs really started to escalate. The rejected goods had to be scrapped, stored, accounted for, reworked or in some other way either brought up to standard or treated as waste. This took time and resources and it added nothing in terms of value.

At the same time, the culture in the organisation was one where quality was someone else's issue, where individuals knew they could rely on someone else to find the problems, so they could bash on and build in the odd mistake and error. The emphasis was on quantity, not quality, and the payment system led to people cutting corners to achieve bonuses and piecework rates. The management style was frequently about keeping people at their own tasks, deliberately limiting their involvement in any other areas of the organisation, and working through top-down instructions and orders.

Most crucially, nobody examined what was going wrong with a view to preventing it happening again. There were no processes for learning from past mistakes and establishing ways of improving quality at every stage, continuously. After all, it wasn't in the quality inspectors' interests for everyone to get it right all the time. The expected error rate meant that 96% was fine and all the attention went on picking over what had already been done, and sorting out existing mistakes.

Being separated parts of a chain, one department neither knew nor cared what effect its producing sub-standard goods had on the next link in the chain. Problems and mistakes were treated as causes for interdepartmental strife rather than co-operation, with blame and negative conflict being far more prevalent than teamwork across departmental boundaries.

We could go on, but you should have a clear enough picture by now.

Modern quality management

Today, quality is about continuous improvement, and everyone working to identify ways of getting closer and closer to the required standard. Phrases like:

'zero defects'

'right first time'

'fit for its purpose'

replace the 96% right approach.

To achieve this, management has to demonstrate its own clear commitment, and has to develop teams within the organisation, cutting across the traditional demarcations and divisions between separate processes. The implications of one person's failure on the work of others further down the production chain are seen as crucially important, and everyone is responsible for their own quality. This requires training and awareness raising, with a drive towards opening up communication at every level between front line workers and managers.

In addition, everyone is encouraged to help improve any part of the operations, and to feel empowered by the responsibility and trust that is placed in them.

One more point before we move on. Our focus has been on quality as a simple example, but ask any successful organisation in any field about its culture, and you will find the same sort of underlying characteristics in place. Quality management is just good management, and is equally valid in health and safety management.

Links with health and safety

You may recognise some of the traditional quality management issues in health and safety, either where you work now or somewhere you have been in the past. Unfortunately, even in organisations that have espoused modern quality techniques, the approach to health and safety can lag a long way behind.

The trigger for any health and safety action is still often an accident or incident. There is no planning for continuous improvement, no team work on preventing problems across departmental boundaries, little or no involvement of people in the vital aspects of what they do and how they do it safely.

Any accident leads to blame, recrimination, and a 'cover your back' approach, and if that means another department carries the can, that's OK. A level of accidents and ill health is regarded as natural and inevitable – like the 96% quality target.

Think about it ...

If you had to choose the 4% of health and safety that could be allowed to go wrong, what would you pick?

In modern health and safety management, zero defects and striving for continuous improvement are built into the system. Teams focus on them, everyone makes a contribution and the people who know most – those actually working in the areas concerned – are treated as experts in their own work.

All in all, effective quality management is so close in character to a sound health and safety culture, that the two are interchangeable.

The benefits of a positive health and safety culture

Organisations where the health and safety culture mirrors what is needed for effective quality management, and health and safety is regarded as an integral component to core business success experience:

- greater co-operation between departments, individuals and levels within the organisation, as everyone works together on what is perceived as an issue of common concern and mutual interest

- empowerment of all staff that raises morale, motivation and commitment to the organisation, as people feel encouraged to contribute to their own and their colleagues' success

- enhanced communication systems and outcomes, with everyone feeling more able to speak up and to listen

- fewer accidents, near-misses and incidents, and reduced levels of occupational ill health – saving costs and enhancing the constructive climate in the workplace

- more problems being solved quickly, quietly and without a lot of fuss, as the ownership of the issues spreads.

HEALTH AND SAFETY AND MANAGEMENT THINKING

In most organisations problem-solving, creative thinking, forecasting and scenario planning (what if …) form a central part of the business planning approach. Managers are expected to think through the factors in the environment that could affect the future success and direction of the organisation, and come up with plans that support the positive factors and tackle the negative ones. You probably know about such forecasting techniques in sales, production, technology and other business areas.

The basic approach is to investigate what is happening in the outside world with a formula like PESTLE, and then making informed guesses about the effects of each factor on the organisation in future.

PESTLE is an acronym for a set of general business forecasting headings:

Political
Economic
Social
Technological
Legal
Environmental.

The approach is to consider what is happening in the world under each heading – say, technological – and identify its impact on the business. So, a new computerised machine may become available in a specialised production area that you work in, and the forecasting could range over the following points:

- *what if* our competitors buy one – what difference will that make to us, our customers and their expectations?
- *what if* we get one – what extra products and services could we offer that the market wants?
- *what if* we didn't get one – would we do enough business with the old machines to justify the financial decision not to buy a new one?
- *what if* the rumours are right, and there's a Mk 2 being developed already – what are the issues in waiting for a better model?

In health and safety, the management approach to forecasting is an exact parallel – questions like:

- what if we do nothing about that problem – what could happen?
- what would be the ramifications of that?
- what if I did this – how would the various parties react?

Forecasting is not planning. It is a best guess, based on information and experience. With a bit of creative thinking it helps inform plans. It is never an exact science, as you know from the fact that the weather is forecast and not planned, but it is an essential element in businesses that know where they fit in the wider environment and plan to take advantage of developments, or control the effects of adverse factors.

There is a point here about the fundamentally different way we want you to look at health and safety. If your only health and safety concerns are about people not complying with instructions then you're not being creative and reflective enough. Sure, rules and regulations are an important issue, but they are about implementing today's plans, not revising them and looking forward creatively. But forecasting doesn't have to be complicated or technically demanding. Often it is the simple issues that can be tackled first, in some cases by identifying ways of getting people to conform by taking a different tack.

Forecasting here is about thinking through the results of your actions, so you can anticipate their effects. It may mean coming at a problem from an entirely different angle, while remembering the importance of the 'So what' selling technique. It is a management problem-solving technique that applies to health and safety just as much as to any other managerial problem.

The first principle is to change the way you approach the problem. To paraphrase Edward de Bono, who writes on creative thinking:

> *If you know something is buried two feet down and you've dug down three feet without finding it – stop digging there and dig somewhere else.*

Hard hats

On a large construction site there were constant problems with workers neglecting to wear the hats with which they had been provided. Repeated instructions and threats were having little or no effect, although in the past there had never seemed to be a problem.

The site manager considered the implications. Broadly, they were legal and practical. Legally he, individual workers and the company could be in trouble if an inspector spotted the lack of hats. More seriously, there was a major legal problem if someone was hurt while not wearing their hat. Practically and ethically, it was someone's life at stake if something fell from the scaffolding and struck a worker – not to mention the effect on the person up the scaffolding who had dropped it. Rather than keep pushing at the same door, the site manager thought through the problem and did some investigation, asking people why they were so reluctant to wear the hats.

The main problem was that they were all in bright luminescent colours that the workers thought were cissy. In addition, they said they were not nearly as comfortable and light as the hats they used to wear, and they were having a negative impact on the amount of work people could do. Bricklayers, for instance, were finding that their performance (and their bonus) was down as a result of having to adjust the hats constantly and take them off for a short break (and a moan about them). These answers seemed so trite and inconsequential that he didn't at first believe they mattered. However, he confirmed for himself that this was really what the workers felt and recognised that to them the perception was the reality, whatever the facts of the matter. The company had changed its hat supplier, and the workers simply didn't like the way the new hats felt.

He asked himself:

- *what if I do nothing*
  and recognised the problems this would cause, and that they were unacceptable

- *what if I get different hats but they're still in these colours*
  and knew that they still wouldn't wear them

▶

▶

- *what if I tell them they must wear them*
  and recognised this hadn't worked so far, and there was no reason to assume it would start working now
- *what if I ask for more expensive hats from the company*
  and realised they needed sound reasons to change back – reasons that mattered to them, not just that he was having difficulty getting people to wear the hats
- *what if I do get the old hats back*
  and realised he could increase his popularity and use the situation to insist they play their part and wear them, once he'd done his part

The site manager told some key workers on the site grapevine that he was trying to change the supplier back for them, so the colour problem was removed. He then put up a very different case to his bosses – one based purely on financial forecasts. His central argument was the benefits of reverting to the old hats, as the few pounds saved on the price were less than the costs it led to. He showed that lost production alone cost more than the savings made on hats. Add to that the cost of a prosecution, an inspector stopping work or an accident and the costs would massively outweigh the savings. He didn't argue on colour, knowing that his bosses would simply instruct him to tell the workers to put up with it and stop being stupid, because he knew this would only make matters worse.

The company, with an eye to the benefits and the costs, replaced the hats and the problem was solved. A potentially serious health and safety issue had been nipped in the bud by some research, some creative thinking, some forecasting and some simple management psychology.

In this example the manager has played the benefit card and stressed the factors that matter to each party. He has thought through the implications and taken a creative view of the problems. In the end the action was simple, but effective.

So, developing a positive approach to health and safety is just as much good business sense and practice as is preventive maintenance, or buildings and contents insurance. It is more than enforcing rules and regulations – it's about the balance between costs and benefits, and the implications of doing something weighed against not doing it.

All that needs to happen is that action is taken to remove or reduce a potential risk to health or safety as soon as it is recognised. But here is the crux of the issue. How do we get people to take that step towards prevention rather than mopping up afterwards?

Think about it ...

What specifically will turn your top managers on to a more positive approach to health and safety?

You need to ask this question, so that you can plan to help them raise the level of their own commitment, through issues that matter to them. It could be money, personal status, company image – it really doesn't matter. What matters is that you know which buttons to press to get them started. One answer lies in the link between corporate business policy and the role health and safety plays at that central level.

1

Policy and practice

The foundations for improvement have been laid in the analysis of costs and benefits. If the board of directors, for instance, accepts that poor health and safety is an issue that affects the core business then it's likely to issue some sort of policy statement – something on the lines of:

> *It is our policy that health and safety must be given priority in the operations of our business, as a positive contribution to the well-being and development of the people working here and the organisation as a whole.*

Pretty general stuff, really, but that's what policy is, and that's what directors are there to do – devise policy that takes the organisation forward. They're not there to do the detailed work of departmental managers or those running smaller sections. This operational and tactical level of work is the remit of middle and junior managers, whose task is to translate policy into action that means the policy is delivered. You need both policy and a means of implementation.

But whoever issues the policy has to mean it. If it's worth saying, it's worth saying with conviction. An effective policy is worthwhile, whereas one that doesn't work in practice is a waste of time and space. There's nothing very revolutionary about this, of course, but look at the health and safety policy in some organisations and it's a meaning-less jumble of words with no practical application. The only reason there is a policy at all is that the law says there has to be, so they copy one from another organisation or give it to someone relatively junior to cobble together.

A sound policy must come from the top and proclaim the genuine commitment of the organisation. It must set high expectations and encourage people to believe that it can be achieved, given effort.

However, the policy must be rooted in a practical context. It's point-less having a policy without the building blocks essential to real progress – things like adequate resources, clear knowledge of the rel-evant codes of practice and a vision of the health and safety standards to which the organisation is to operate.

Then there must be a strategy and tactics to make it work. Without a detailed plan for implementation nothing gets done and the policy loses touch with reality. In the early days of equal opportunities, for example, many organisations used to say in their advertising that:

> *we are committed to equality of opportunity, and to employing the best people regardless of gender, race, colour or religion.*

Unfortunately, it didn't work in many cases. The policy had been approved because it was a current issue that concerned organisations. Many said it simply because they didn't want to be left out. But the resources needed to make it happen weren't in place and inadequate thought had been given to how to make it a reality. Nobody had been given the job of turning the policy into a series of detailed plans that could be implemented, so it stayed as a series of fine words. Not a parsnip was buttered.

Strategic components

To implement a policy there have to be certain strategic elements in place. These include:

- a clear understanding of who is responsible
- some measurable and achievable objectives
- standards and codes of practice to work to, setting the ethical and practical framework for acceptable operational levels and outcomes
- adequate resources

- a plan of action
- training to develop the necessary skills, knowledge and understanding of everyone involved
- review procedures to check on how things are going and to identify what has improved, or what still needs to be improved.

You will spend some time at the end of the book, looking at what you can do in your own organisation to develop an appropriate strategy that takes account of these and/or other relevant issues.

Towards a healthy and safe organisation

Two colleagues were having a drink at the end of a day's managing.

'The only acceptable target is zero defects. That's a tenet of quality management and it's just as central to health and safety. One accident, one person suffering ill-health, is one too many.'

'That's all well and good, but accidents happen. If you could prevent them they wouldn't be accidents. All right, you can possibly stop some of them, but to aim for 100% is impossible. Anyway, you're always on about health and safety.'

'So, which people are we supposed to allow to suffer? Which ones do we expect to get hurt and what do we plan for?'

'You're twisting my words. I didn't say it was something you plan – but there are some really dangerous areas at work and they tend to have the highest potential for accidents. The loading bay, for instance, with all the lorries backing in and out, and the fork lift trucks on the move.'

'Fair point. It is more risky down there. But how do we cover other business risks… things like potential bad debts? We look at the records to identify where the problems might come up, and then try and put most attention where it's needed.'

'That's a totally different issue. You can spot most of the likely bad debts – they're either the same people who always pay late, or firms with similar characteristics to those we've had problems with before.'

'Yes. Precisely. And we can do the same thing with health and safety.'

'Oh, don't go on. Accidents happen – they can't be predicted. It's all down to luck. Damn – I've spilt my drink. I knew I'd do that if I sat at this table… its got wonky legs and it always happens!'

WHAT ARE WE TALKING ABOUT?

Words have a powerful effect. Choosing the wrong word can convey an image different to what was intended. Sometimes, too, common words and phrases lose their meaning because of overuse, or the way they get used as a sort of shorthand. So, what does health and safety mean? What do the words represent? You know when you say a word over and over again and it loses both its meaning and its shape – well, *healthandsafety* has become a bit like that for a lot of managers. It's a catch-all phrase that has lost its real meaning for many people, representing an aspect of the job which is now almost part of the furniture. It's just always there, in every job description and every book about management, so it gets taken for granted and down-valued.

Let's explore the words a little, before looking at the key issues in more depth. Maybe the way to focus on the construction of a positive health and safety culture is to break away from just 'health and safety' and to add something. What we're really targeting is *improving* or *developing* health and safety, so perhaps one of those words could go at the front?

'One of my responsibilities is improving health and safety.'

'My management role includes the need to develop health and safety.'

Even the term 'management' implies control and the maintenance of the status quo. The aim is to get beyond that, changing people's thinking and attacking the problem.

'Health' is another word that gets passed over, on the way to safety. The health side of the equation merits a mention, because it receives far too little attention. This is despite the fact that it is a major source of organisational problems and potentially a crippling disability to the people who suffer from ill health as a result of their work.

Health

Mention health and safety and what springs to mind for most people are gory accidents, lost limbs and moving machinery. But preventing ill health from occupational sources is just as important as preventing accidents at work. It certainly matters as much to the people who suffer its results – ask anyone who can no longer work as the result of a lung or skin disorder.

Ill health is also statistically a bigger problem that accidents – more people die each year from work-related disease than from accidents at work.

The main characteristics that distinguish health from accidents are suddenness and visibility. Chemicals and other substances are just one cause. For example, someone who has worked for years in an occupation where fibreglass is used can develop respiratory problems, but these may not emerge for a long time and are not visible to the naked eye. And resins, glues and paints are just the tip of the iceberg.

It may surprise and even shock you to know that three quarters of all trainees in hairdressing under Youth Training in 1991 had skin conditions that were measurably worse while they were are work. These were young people, maybe your children and your friends' children, not long out of school and already with problems that would affect the rest of their working lives. Not every one of the trainees had dermatitis, and not every case can be blamed specifically on hairdressing. But dermatitis is quite prevalent and can be brought on by certain chemicals that are used in bleaching, perming and styling hair. In other industries, oils and solvents, weather and working conditions, and even having to wash the hands frequently and remove the skin's natural protection can be contributing factors to skin disorders like dermatitis.

Asbestos is perhaps the most widely-known factor in lung and other disorders. It is clearly linked to cancer and is now a well-known health hazard the effects of which are no secret. Exposure to it is now strictly controlled by regulation, but the vast majority of problems arise from contact with it years ago.

Environmental issues can be a problem too; for instance, noise causes deafness – the annual HSE figures have a section for noise-related ill health. And perhaps one of the fastest growing areas of occupational ill-health – stress – is one that managers will find it easy to relate to.

So, health is a major element in the whole equation, but it is easier to forget because, for example, you can't see deafness and it doesn't generally happen overnight. It's also the sort of issue that managers can put off, because it isn't going to stop the work today or tomorrow.

This can make it a hard topic to use in examples in a book like this one, so we could be accused of putting too much emphasis on accidents at the expense of health. However, we are aware of the problem and have at least come out and pleaded guilty, with mitigating circumstances.

Think about it ...

What areas of employees' health are most at risk where you work? If you can't come up with any ideas, have a chat with the personnel manager or the person who does the required returns for HSE. It might surprise you.

A couple of health-related issues have been a focus of attention recently. COSSH which looks at the control and use of substances that could damage users' and others' health is one. Another is the European directive on visual display screens and units, and the regulations to protect those working at them. We're not going to go into long explanations of the rules and regulations, so if you want to find out more about what's involved and what your organisation should be doing, get in touch with HSE and they'll send you plenty of information.

Accidents

What, to you, is an accident? How would you define it?

Accidents are defined in the HSE booklet *Successful Health and Safety Management* as:

> *... any undesired circumstances which give rise to ill health or injury, damage to property, plant, products or the environment, production losses or increased liabilities.*

In other words, an accident is an unplanned event or events that lead to harm, injury or damage. However, the fact that it is unplanned does not make it unavoidable, so let's dispense with any comments like 'accidents do happen'. Granted, there are situations where acts of God impact on the organisation and what it does, but in the vast majority of cases accidents are predictable and preventable.

Incidents

Incidents can help prevent accidents – as long as the systems are in place to learn from past experience and take appropriate corrective action. You remember in the last chapter, we looked at quality as an issue which links to health and safety, and this prevention through analysis of past problems was a central point.

Incidents are accidents that don't cause damage, harm or injury. That's the only difference and it is down to luck, this time. The luck comes into it because the hammer that falls from the top of the construction site doesn't hit anyone or anything when it lands, so nobody does anything about it. Luck is all that makes the difference when the filing cabinet tips over and falls harmlessly on the floor, instead of on a human being.

Think about it ...

Is there any real difference between a drunk driver who hits someone and one who narrowly misses them?

2

In one way, yes of course there is. Someone got hurt by the first one. But clearly there's not a scrap of difference between the potential for each to maim or kill someone – they're both accidents looking for somewhere to happen. The first one just met someone who was unlucky enough to be in the wrong place. The other one's turn will come. So the principles don't change, and the measures that society takes to control and handle the mixture of alcohol and lethal weapons like cars are basically constant.

The question is whether the same amount of attention is given to incidents – near misses – as is given to accidents that do harm. It's a rhetorical question really, because it never is. Yet the information that an incident provides is just as relevant as the results of an accident, in its usefulness for planning and prevention through continuous improvement – and it is a lot more available. A survey a few years ago showed the following breakdown. For every fatal or serious injury, there were:

- 3 minor injuries (with the worker off sick for up to three days)
- 50 injuries requiring first-aid

- 80 accidents causing property damage
- 400 incidents that caused no damage or injury – so-called 'near misses'.

PREVENTION

> *If it walks like a duck, looks like a duck, lays eggs, has feathers and quacks – it could be a duck.*
>
> Attributed to President George Bush

In other words, if something happens enough times it is likely to happen again. The chances are there is an inherent problem. Whether it's a series of accidents or incidents, or a mixture of both, the key to preventing a recurrence is to work through the steps in the routine that follows.

As with any problem-solving technique, it works best when a multi-functional team drawn from a range of levels looks at the issues, because a team can:

- include people with specialist knowledge
- spark off creative thinking, when someone develops a basic idea someone else starts off
- share ownership of the issue and disseminate information to different parts of the organisation
- co-ordinate solutions and plans and share the workload.

It also demonstrates your and the organisation's commitment to opening up health and safety as a corporate and common issue, to sharing information and responsibility in an empowering way and to listening to the ideas of people at all levels of the hierarchy.

A simple routine for reducing the chance of it happening again

Ask yourself for a number of similar incidents:

- What happened?
- When?
- Where?
- Why?
- Why else?
- Who was involved?
- What common factors emerge from this analysis?
- Which are relevant and which aren't?
- Which are easiest, cheapest and quickest to tackle?
- What's the correlation between relevance and ease?
- What shall we do immediately and over a longer time period to cut the odds of it happening again?

2

In both serial and individual situations, the same sort of approach can help identify not only what has happened but also what is likely to happen – a sort of forecast. There are some tips to using it, which include:

- never jump to conclusions before you have analysed everything – if the first couple of incidents have a common pattern, don't assume that the others do as well; they may do, but assuming anything in health and safety is dangerous

- most accidents and incidents are not the result of a single factor – they occur because several factors come into play at the same time; the difference between an accident and an incident is probably one factor

- keep asking the question 'Why?' until you get to the real heart of the problem – and ask 'Why else?' to find out all the contributing factors

- when it comes to exploring the relevance and ease of the factors, it isn't always the costliest or the most difficult that have the greatest potential impact

- always look for ways to improve the general situation; don't just say it was a certain person and they're always a danger – identify what they do that causes the problem and then work on ways of designing that out of the system or procedure

- wherever possible (and it usually is) include people who were there and who were directly involved – they tend to know best what is going on

- wherever it is appropriate and possible, open up the discussion as widely as you can, so that everyone feels they own part of the problem and can share in the solution

- if using a team, keep the number to no more than seven; eight people can start to turn into two teams or factions, or into a committee.

It is essential to keep asking the question, 'Why?' This is so that you can identify the real central issues and causes and not just the symptoms of a problem.

The filing cabinet

A filing cabinet in a garage toppled over and injured an employee. The people involved – manager, clerk, mechanics who came in and used the files – all sat round and used the routine. They established that the cabinet tipping forward was a problem that had been an incident before, but had been caught and pushed back in place just in time, several times. It had happened to several people and on various occasions, so no real pattern emerged there. Then they asked why, and why else.

Why?
Because it was loaded up in such a way that the top was heavier than the bottom.

Why?
Because it's easier to stuff things in the top drawer than to bend down and use the lower drawers.

Why?
Because the cabinet is tucked away behind the desk and it's a tight squeeze.

Why?
Well, no real reason – it's just always been there.

Why else?
Because the bottom drawer wasn't opened (as we all know it should be) to stabilise the cabinet.

Why?
The same reasons – it is tucked away behind the desk.

From this persistent analysis emerged some really simple factors. The principal one was the location of the cabinet. It was in such a position that people couldn't – even if they wanted to – take the appropriate steps to ensure the cabinet's safety.

The solution initially was to replace the cabinet (the old one had been broken in the accident) with one which had built-in safety mechanisms that prevented a recurrence, and to move it out from behind the desk to a blank wall. Then the clerk rearranged the contents of the cabinet so they were spread through all the drawers. Had they been able to use the old cabinet, a few extra precautions would have been needed.

2

> **Think about it ...**
>
> *If they had moved the old cabinet to a new position, what extra precautions could have been appropriate to prevent a recurrence?*

Staff had lost the habit of opening drawers in the right order, to stabilise the cabinet, so if the old one had been moved to a new position a five minute training session would have been useful, to ensure everyone knew the safe operating procedure. A large notice on the wall over the cabinet would have been a permanent reminder to everyone to do it properly and take their time.

Another option would have been to control the cabinet's use, either limiting it to a few members of staff, or making one person responsible for monitoring its safe use. In the extreme, the manager could have said that anyone found using the cabinet wrongly was subject to immediate disciplinary action – but this rather heavy-handed approach may be best kept in reserve for special cases. Getting everyone involved instead of threatening them is likely to have far more positive outcomes.

The way they approached the issue was through the routine, getting everyone involved in the problem, the solution, and the training afterwards. In developing a positive health and safety culture, the way forward is not to meet behind closed doors and issue a revised procedure based on the deliberations of a few managers.

What they got wrong was to ignore the warning signs when the cabinet tipped forward on other occasions, but didn't actually cause any harm or damage. The underlying reason for tackling problems in this way should, by now, be clear to you. It is for much bigger reasons than simply being seen to do something. It should be to prevent accidents and ill health that will otherwise cause real problems for the organisation and the individual. In Chapter 1 you had a look at some of the underlying costs and benefits in the equation, so what are the real financial and other costs?

THE COSTS OF NOT GETTING HEALTH AND SAFETY RIGHT

Getting health and safety wrong is hugely expensive in financial terms, for the nation, for the organisation and for the individual.

The national scene

National statistics aren't always very meaningful in their raw form. But the sheer scale of time and money lost and distress caused through injury and ill health just has to be mentioned. We'll do it in a way that you may find worth developing in your own advocacy of a positive health and safety culture. Turning raw data into understandable examples and pictures can make it a lot more powerful.

Thirty million working days a year are lost through ill health and work-related injuries. That's a fact – and it's so big it is virtually beyond meaning for those of us who can't comprehend thirty million. So, how about saying that this is ten times the number of days lost in strikes? Does that make it more powerful? Or how about saying that:

- it's far more than the number of working days lost if 100,000 workers were made redundant and didn't work for a whole year

- if you assume as a rough average that you work 200 days a year (5 days x 40 weeks, with the rest accounted for in weekends, Bank

Holiday and annual leave) then you would have to work for 150,000 years to put in that number of days

- it is equivalent to 3,000 people – the working population of a small market town – never working in a generous working life span of 50 years.

Another example for any managers who are concerned only with the bottom line, could be that allowing an annual salary of £15,000 and adding on conservative employment costs of, say, another £5,000, the cost of these lost days comes out at three billion (thousand million) pounds.

The organisational picture

In this section on the organisation we shall look at two areas of cost. The first area is immediate financial costs – all of them – that are incurred if an accident happens and just one person who is crucial to your operations is off work for a few weeks.

2

The pressing problem

In an engineering works in the Midlands, one worker specialised in high grade parts for special applications. He used an expensive and specialist machine that machined components at extreme speed and sometimes under high pressure. Because of the dangers involved there were strict controls, including a light beam that was broken if anyone came too close to the moving parts. It turned the machine off if anyone broke it and it was a requirement that it was always on when the machine was running. In fact, the machine was designed so it couldn't be tampered with or adjusted without being turned off.

But this was an engineering works, and they found a way round it. The operator depended on high production levels to get the bonus up, so he developed a way of disengaging the light beam and then removing dust and other debris from the danger area without stopping the machine. It saved several minutes downtime between operations. The supervisor knew it had been happening for some time, but nothing had gone wrong and the pressure was on for production to complete a trial order for a new and important client. In any event, the supervisor knew that senior management would not back him, so a blind eye was turned.

The inevitable happened. A moment's inattention and the operator's

▶

▶

hand was caught. The hand and forearm went in a flash, although the rest of the arm was saved after a lengthy session of surgery.

The shop floor was shut down immediately. Everyone was in a state of shock, and emergency meetings went on in the board room. The Factory Inspector closed the operation down, pending immediate improvements and an investigation, and the whole firm – especially the managers who spent massive amounts of time meeting to discuss it between themselves, completing claim forms, and talking to lawyers and insurance people – was preoccupied with the accident for weeks.

Relations between management, the other employees and their union representatives became very creaky. The order with the potential new client had to be fulfilled, but they got to hear about it and placed no further business the firm's way. And the man, in hospital without an arm, his family around him, recognised he wouldn't work again so he sued them for tens of thousands ... and won a significant part of the claim.

The firm was prosecuted and fined very heavily and their insurers nearly managed to escape any liability at all, because the terms of the policy were breached by the over-riding of the light beam. All in all, it put the organisation back several years, from a position where it had been a rising star in the local business world, to one where it had to pick itself up and start virtually from scratch.

The costs of an accident at work like this one are much greater than you might think. They include the following:

● lost production on the equipment or machinery involved – in the example, production of specialist production of items with a high profit margin and potential for business expansion if the contract went well

● lost production arising from the department being closed down temporarily, by the firm while it sorts out the mess and/or by the Factory Inspectorate who can issue prohibition notices

● sick pay for the individual

● costs of overtime for others to make up the shortfall, or the costs of getting in someone short-term, on contract or from an agency – assuming you can find someone at short notice with the skills to replace the one who is off sick, which in the example was not possible

● sub-contracting the work out to another firm at premium rates (almost ransom rates because the need is so urgent, and the firm in the example had no alternative), in order to comply with the delivery terms of a contract rather than face swingeing financial penalties

- any legal penalties and fines that might arise

- the costs of repairing and replacing the machine – not just the purchase costs, but the costs of getting the damage sorted out, the old machine moved and the new one installed

- compensation, from any claims by the employee

- the hidden financial costs of spending hours investigating and recording what happened, holding meetings, preparing all the paperwork for an investigation, interviews with inspectors, insurance assessors, union people and others

- the rise in insurance premiums, this year and every other year.

Get the picture? It starts to mount up as you add in all the hidden costs that you may have forgotten, or would like to forget.

And it hasn't finished yet, because there are other, even more subtle costs that affect the bottom line, things like:

- reduced output from other workers whose morale and performance drops away – even to the point of dismissal in some cases (such as the supervisor in the example, who lost his job for gross misconduct, as a result of the accident) or resignation in others (like the production manager in the example who couldn't return to the shop floor and live with the emotional trauma and guilt)

- damage to the firm's reputation inside and outside, through publicity which affects relationships with customers and the perceptions of the best potential employees – the ones you want to attract in future

- any penalties that come from not fulfilling orders on time

- opportunity costs, like while you're catching up the lost production, you can't take on new orders and expand the business

- failures in delivery because production is disrupted, that undermine the company's normal reliability in the eyes of its customers.

Now ask yourself in the light of what you read in Chapter 1 – how many of these costs can we claim back through insurance? Not many, in virtually every case. Statistically, something under 10% of the total lost by firms through accidents and ill health is claimable under insurance.

The second area of costs is the broad cost of not developing the organisation so it stays at the leading edge in an increasingly competitive world. These costs can be hard to quantify, but by looking at the benefits of a positive reputation for health and safety, you can infer the downside of the same equation. In other words, where effective health and safety encourages high quality job applications, the downside is that a poor reputation encourages a lower quality, as the best candidates go for jobs with what they see as the best companies. The net result is lower quality human resources, which cost money in reduced output and increased training needs, to name just two areas.

There is a direct relationship between health and safety policies and culture; the overall culture in other areas of activity and the level of corporate success. Organisations that ignore this relationship risk incurring broad costs by losing out in a competitive world to organisations that develop integrated approaches across the range of corporate activity.

Health and safety is a mainstream business area, not least because there are other mainstream areas of business thinking on which health and safety policies have an impact and where a positive approach can reduce or minimise costs. Just a few examples are:

- finance, where insurance, health and safety failure costs and all the other issues you are looking at in detail here play a vital part in cost reduction
- human resource management, where an organisation with a sound health and safety culture:
    - benefits from high quality applicants who want to join the best companies, available for recruitment and selection
    - experiences lower turnover and higher retention rates, thus reducing recruitment costs, loss of skills and expertise, training costs of new staff and so on
    - has better communications systems and greater job satisfaction, encouraging better production, higher quality and fewer problems
- product design and liability, where product specification, international standards and the Consumer Protection Act all relate closely to health and safety policy and culture
- operations management, where quality management is a key issue

in maximising the amount of added value, and cutting waste

● environmental and waste management, high profile issues that are under increasing public scrutiny.

There are many other such areas, and the key point is that failing to relate health and safety to other business thinking inevitably costs money and other resources. It may be harder to measure than the immediate costs of an accident, but because it is deeper-rooted, embedded in the culture and cutting across every part of the organisation's way of working the level of cost tends to be much higher – and always there.

Incidentally, if you want more evidence of the real costs of poor health and safety, either the specific and immediately measurable ones or the deeper and longer term ones, ask the Health and Safety Executive. They will send you all sorts of hard information and extremely helpful material that will prove the point beyond any doubt whatsoever. They will even come and talk to you about it, and you'll find that their approach is increasingly one where they work with you, to help you develop a positive culture, instead of waiting for things to go wrong and then naming the guilty parties.

The individual

Any organisation that doesn't care about its people will not be worried about the costs to an individual employee who suffers as a result of the firm's poor health and safety approach. But very few organisations believe or would admit that they have an employee relations policy that demonstrates no concern at all for their employees as people. Successful organisations recognise that their employee relations approach has a direct bearing on the bottom line, through motivation, performance, attracting and retaining the best people, and generally developing a good reputation as an employer. Therefore, it is another aspect of the win/win situation, where both employer and employee benefit from success in health and safety.

The best way to look at this financially is for you to imagine what it would cost you to be off work. In some cases there won't be a major direct cost, if it's a short-term absence, because the company may make arrangements to keep your pay up, at least for a set period. But the sad truth is that out of sight quickly means out of mind.

> ***Think about it ...***
>
> *Cast your mind back and remember old what's-their-name, the person who went sick and eventually just disappeared from the scene. I wonder what happened to them and what they're doing now?*

If it's permanent – some injury that means you can't do your last job any more – what then? What about the loss of earnings? Think about the YTS trainees in hairdressing. What are the chances of any of them picking up another career if dermatitis halts their tonsorial activities? And you, as someone who bought this book, you're more likely to have an established life style that is threatened – mortgage to pay, school costs, and all the rest.

But the costs don't stop there, of course. Special diets, attendance, nursing and medical treatment don't always come cheap, and as anyone who ends up confined to a wheelchair will tell you, houses need to be adapted – wider doors, rails in the toilet, shower and bed-room. Stairs, of course, are now out of the question.

And the emotional trauma that comes with injury is massive and virtually unquantifiable. These non-financial costs are worth a close look in their own right.

The non-financial costs

So what are the other costs? Well, they're emotional and personal costs.

> ***Think about it ...***
>
> *What would it cost you if you lost the sight of one eye in an accident at work?*
>
> *What would it cost you if you had to tell someone else that their father or partner, who worked for you, had lost the sight of one eye in an accident at work?*
>
> *What would it cost you if you witnessed an accident where someone lost their sight?*

It doesn't bear thinking about. You may have said something about the financial costs of not being able to work again having lost an eye, but it's more the emotional costs that surface here. These costs are not measurable in financial terms – they're on a different scale entirely. The chances are that nobody involved in an accident like this would ever be the same again. Certainly, the person who lost an eye wouldn't, but neither would someone who was married to them, who called them Mum or Dad, or who had to tell the family about it.

After an accident like this, the common cry goes up 'if only'. If only the money had been spent on that guard screen, if only they had been wearing the eye protection, if only we had done something about it earlier … But it's too late then, and the emotional costs live on long after the financial costs have been paid and accounted for.

The problem is that whenever someone says, 'if only', it almost certainly means that the problem was known about and nothing was done. Interestingly, the problem also provides the solution. If you think about the shift in perspective we talked about in the previous chapter and the emphasis placed on learning about prevention from analysing accidents and incidents, it starts to become a lot clearer.

THE COSTS OF A POSITIVE HEALTH AND SAFETY APPROACH

If you see the development of a positive approach to health and safety as an investment, it certainly has costs. Again, we can draw a parallel with quality management, where the analysis of costs is a powerful tool for progress.

In quality management, the costs of not taking a positive approach include all the issues you saw listed in Chapter 1 – things like:

- the cost of scrapped products and materials
- the cost of reworking or repairing substandard items
- replacement costs of equipment, plant, machinery and materials
- the costs of employing inspectors to find, investigate and control poor output
- the costs of moving, storing, recording, accounting for, administering all the materials that are being rejected

- the lost production that goes on putting mistakes right
- the opportunity costs that come from people and equipment being tied up in producing scrap in the first place and then reworking it, that prevents the organisation using that capacity to take on new business, expand or develop new products
- all the costs of investigation, meetings, reports that blame other people.

The costs of developing a positive quality culture and approach include training, awareness raising, meetings that have to take place to identify improvements, maybe better rewards for employees who come up with cost-effective solutions. It may be necessary to prime the pump, and get in a consultant to kick-start the motor driving the pump, and that isn't necessarily cheap.

The parallel with developing the health and safety culture means that the costs include:

- the costs of training people in safe working systems
- the costs of awareness raising, maybe through meetings, so that everyone's commitment to health and safety grows
- better facilities, better rest rooms and a greater degree of visible welfare for staff
- the costs of making equipment safer
- first aid training.

The question is – how to justify these costs?

The economic balance

It has been estimated by business statisticians that up to 40% of an organisation's turnover can be wasted on activities like those in the list of failure costs, work that produces nothing, adds no value but does add costs. You have already looked at the nature and extent of costs and waste resulting from poor health and safety – so what about the costs of developing the culture and the operations? How do you justify spending even more?

The point is that you only spend more for the short term at most. Investing resources in developing the culture is like planned preventive maintenance – it stops machines breaking down so the investment is judged to be worthwhile. It's like having a faulty fuel system that reduces the miles per gallon you get from a car. In the short term it costs more to get it sorted out, but as soon as it is running it goes on saving for years and years, with the savings increasing as the price of fuel goes up. The way forward is to analyse and compare the costs on each side of the equation, the costs of failure and the costs of prevention. Somewhere in the equation between these sets of costs is an optimum point of economic balance, where the lowest realistic expenditure produces the best return.

This is why you need to start from the top, because in the early days there will be a potential rise in costs. There's no point in denying it, but there is a point in justifying it. The point is that once the culture change has started, it develops its own momentum and begins to operate more cheaply, with increasingly better results at the expense of the costs of failure. And you can always take heart that you're spending money where the law asks you to focus, so you win both ways.

SOME BASIC HEALTH AND SAFETY PRINCIPLES

In this chapter we've made several references to doing it right, but we haven't specified what that means. It should be possible to assume that everyone knows the basics of health and safety, at the level where it complies with the law and with good practice, but as assumptions can be dangerous, a look at the basic principles – the minimum acceptable level of action – is worthwhile. If you think you know the basics, have a read through anyway, just to confirm you are right.

Everything we advocate as a progressive approach to health and safety culture builds on the basic principles. What changes is not the basics, but the way they are applied, the level of management commitment to them and the way they are implemented. Therefore, you will see the basics cropping up in later chapters – you may even recognise one or two from what you have read already. However, rather than preach at you, the information is presented initially as a multiple choice quiz, so you can try out your knowledge and see what you really do know.

HEALTH AND SAFETY MATTERS

1. Organisations that must have a health and safety policy are:
   a) those engaged in manufacturing
   b) those with more than ten employees
   c) those with more than four employees
   d) everyone.

2. Risk assessment is:
   a) always to be carried out by a qualified health and safety officer
   b) being discussed as a possible legal requirement
   c) already a legal requirement in firms with five or more employees
   d) already a legal requirement for manufacturing firms.

3. Organisations employing anyone:
   a) must
   b) should
   c) are recommended to
   d) are free to decide if they want to
   have Employers' Liability Insurance.

4. Displaying the health and safety law poster (or issuing the leaflet):
   a) is a legal requirement
   b) is recommended good practice
   c) covers up damp patches on the wall
   d) means that health and safety becomes an employee responsibility.

5. If management employs a health and safety officer to explain and train people in health and safety procedures:
   a) the responsibility shifts from management to employees
   b) the responsibility is still wholly management's
   c) the responsibility is allocated to everyone, differently
   d) the responsibility rests with the health and safety manager.

6. Recording and notifying the relevant authorities of relevant events, injuries and occupational illnesses is:
   a) optional
   b) mandatory for manufacturing firms
   c) applicable to organisations with more than 20 employees
   d) required legally of every organisation.

7. An organisation with appointed union safety representatives which wants to change a practice that affects health and safety:
   a) is at liberty to take corporate decisions on whether to consult the union representatives
   b) is recommended to involve and consult with them
   c) is required to inform them in detail, no later than ten working days after the change comes into effect
   d) must consult them in advance.

8. In terms of the physical environment, buildings, windows and stairs that are in poor repair, dirty or broken:
   a) have to have an appropriate hazard sign put in a prominent position
   b) can be ignored as long as workers are informed of their condition and given clear advice on the care to be taken
   c) must be repaired
   d) have to be identified in a plan for improvements, with set dates and cost allocations for their upgrading.

9. Clean and well-ventilated toilet facilities, changing facilities where special clothing is worn, and a clean drinking water supply are:
   a) strongly recommended by the Factory Inspectorate
   b) a minimum legal requirement
   c) desirable, where circumstances and the physical layout of building permits
   d) issues the employer can decide whether to provide or not.

10. When using any substances hazardous to health, employers:
    a) are strongly recommended to carry out a risk assessment
    b) must inform employees that they are responsible for investigating the risks themselves, and take no action that jeopardises their health
    c) are deemed to have discharged their legal responsibilities by providing special protective clothing
    d) are required by law to carry out a risk assessment.

2

Don't worry too much if you found bits of the quiz hard to pin down. The positive side of the coin is that you are concerned enough to have a go, and find out. The answers, and a bit of background about each topic, are as follows.

Question 1 – c

The legal answer is that organisations with five or more employees are required to have an up to date health and safety policy. However, there is no reason that all firms shouldn't have one – it is best practice and it clarifies both the commitment and the general organisational thinking, if it is written with care and attention.

A sound policy is linked into other policy areas, as you saw earlier in this chapter. On HSE advice, it should be concerned not only with preventing accidents and ill-health, but also with positive promotion of health and safety. It's the change in perspective, again, from stopping things going wrong, to planning and designing so they go right.

Question 2 – b

Yes, it's a current requirement if you have five or more employees. And it is not just the specialist's role – it is a practice to be carried out and recorded by managers throughout the organisation. There is a fairly strong focus on risk assessment as a contribution to a positive culture, in Chapter 5.

Question 3 – a

Not only does every enterprise that employs someone need to have Employer's Liability insurance – they have to display the certificate as well. It in no way removes or reduces any responsibility that attaches to organisations. All it does is protect employees and others who might suffer at the hands of some employers, and find they could get no compensation.

Question 4 – a

Another legal requirement. You may have one on a wall somewhere where you work. Have you any idea what it says, or what it covers? Possibly not, because for most managers posters like these become part of the wallpaper very quickly.

This is one of the points that is worrying about the traditional approach to health and safety through compulsion. There may be excellent historical reasons for displaying posters like this, and they may be helpful as a reference if anyone has a question that is covered by them. But it can feel as if sticking a poster on a wall is one way of discharging real responsibility. Under the law, it is, but the question has to be asked, what purpose does it really serve?

The worry is that putting up a poster is all some people do, and it is nowhere near enough.

Question 5 – c

Under the Health and Safety At Work Act 1974, employers and employees have their own responsibilities. You saw this in Chapter 1. Broadly, the organisation is responsible for ensuring the health and safety of its employees (full time, part time, casual, temporary, trainees etc.), its visitors, its customers when they use its products or services, people living nearby who may be affected by the processes on the site, the general public … and Uncle Tom Cobley.

Employees have the same sort of responsibility, for the same groups. And managers … well, they get covered from both ends. They are the employer's representatives and they are employees. Be under no illusion – accountability for health and safety cannot be delegated. Employing a specialist, giving someone the job of sorting out your work area, claiming ignorance – all a waste of time when it comes to the crunch.

This very fact is one reason that it makes sense to take a positive approach to health and safety. If you have to do it at all, why not do it well, in a way that brings real benefits for the way the place is managed and organised? Why spend three hours finding ways of not doing something, when doing it only takes an hour and a half in the first place?

Question 6 – d

A legal requirement – so if you don't know what you have to record and notify, find out. If you don't have the evidence, how can you plan improvements based on past experience?

Question 7 – d

Consultation is a must – but here's another legal requirement that can act as a red rag to a bull to some people. Forcing them to consult with what they see as the opposition or the enemy leads to tactical warfare, economy of information and the truth, and conflict instead of co-operation.

Remember, though, the win/win scenario, and the fact that unless everybody wins, nobody wins. We have advocated consultation and involvement from day 1, on everything possible, so restricting it to union representatives and the legal minimum may be a long way short of the ideal. In 99.9% of situations, union representatives are there to achieve the same as you – a safe and healthy working environment. Their motivation may be different, but the outcomes you seek are identical. In the remaining 0.1%, you may need to ask yourself whose fault it is that there appear to be conflicting goals.

Mind you, you have to watch the protocol. If the union has worked hard to appoint and train its representatives, and you go and short-circuit the system without considering their role, status and feelings, you may be right to expect trouble.

Question 8 – c

No debate – employers must provide a safe place of work, and that extends to good repair of buildings, clean and safe stairs and walkways, containers for waste, windows that prevent people falling out of them and safe passage over level floors. There is more – but those are a few examples.

The question to ask yourself is what you expect for yourself, or for one of your family if they were working in the building. The bottom line equation is often best identified by imagining your reactions if one of your children worked in sub-standard conditions.

Question 9 – b

The same basic issues arise here as are covered in question 8.

Question 10 – d

If you missed this one, you may want to think back over the way this book presents health and safety as a management topic that is based not on mopping up after the event, but on preventing problems, cutting mistakes and reducing costs.

Some of the options for answers are designed to look like cop-outs, and if you choose one of those you still have some way to go in developing your own attitude, let alone convincing others.

ATTITUDE PROBLEMS AND THE BASIC PRINCIPLES

The worry is that the legal issues have often in the past been tackled grudgingly and with little or no genuine concern. The approach has sometimes been to see the legal minimum as enough, as the level to be attained, and that's not the way forward with a positive culture.

It may seem a childish way of looking at health and safety, but human beings are remarkably consistent in their reaction to compulsion. Some people love to conform, and do exactly what is required – no less, and unfortunately no more. Other people though, operate the 'not invented here' syndrome, which says if it's someone else's idea it can't be any good, and if it's my idea it must be right. There's a bit of this in everyone, so it may be you recognise it in yourself. If you do, you can tackle it.

However, in developing health and safety you may need to work with other people who have a far more entrenched view than you do. You are then in a psychological area where you have to recognise what motivates people, how to gain their support and commitment, and which buttons to press to turn them on.

2

Maybe you could get them to look at the law in a different way, and see it as a safety net for employees who work for all those other employers who know no better? Maybe a logical approach could open up a positive side to a discussion – after all, the laws and rules are there for a purpose, and what matters is what they are there to achieve, for everyone at work.

The laws have been designed to cope with problems that seemed insoluble through encouragement and cajoling. After all, there are laws on all sorts of issues that you confront every day. The law says you have to have a minimum level of tread on your tyres, but responsible people don't purposely stick at the minimum just because someone else has set down a standard. They act maturely, and decide on levels of safety that they want for themselves and their family and friends as they travel. The law is there to handle the minority who otherwise would not conform – and could cause us harm when they have their accident.

Seen in that light they are both positive and constructive, and should hold no-one back from making real cultural progress.

PLANNING SOME ACTION

At the end of some chapters you will be invited to make some simple plans that will enhance your ability to develop health and safety where you work.

At this point, after two chapters, you have looked at a lot of background information and, as information is power, there may be new areas you need to investigate or issues you have looked at which merit a deeper exploration. The following framework is designed to help you draw your thoughts and ideas together and set yourself some practical steps to take.

ACTION PLAN

The key points I have discovered or confirmed so far are:

_____

_____

_____

_____

My overall aim for health and safety in the organisation is to:

_____

_____

_____

_____

2

The issues that I need to find out more about if I am to achieve the aim are:

_____

_____

_____

_____

... and I can find out more from the following sources:

_____

_____

_____

_____

3

Where are we, and where are we going?

Two colleagues were having a drink at the end of a day's managing.

'See you've got the internal auditors in. How's it going?'

'It's the usual nausea. They keep asking what we did in relation to the policy for purchasing materials and where the evidence is for various things that we bought. It's like I tell them, we have to make it up as we go along sometimes; that's what management is about.'

'Yes, but they're only doing their job. I found them very helpful when I met them. They pointed out where I was likely to go wrong and made some very useful observations about what the policies and procedures really mean for me and the organisation as a whole.'

'You'll learn. The procedures are all very well, but they don't always work, so we have to work round them. So creative accounting pays off – it's the only way to get things done in the end.'

'Surely, though, if a procedure doesn't work it needs changing? You can't just ignore it, and if you don't contribute to reshaping it, it will just get further and further away from reality?'

'The point is, the auditors aren't there to help you get it right in future – their job is to find out what you did wrong in the past and they just want two things. First, they want to catch you out – and it's part of the game to stop them. The other thing they want is to be able to write down that they've checked everything so they're in the clear. The way you're talking you'd think they were on your side!'

'Well, I think they are. I think we're all on the same side – or we should be. After all, all they're looking at is what happens and comparing it with what should happen, working with us to make improvements all round and help the company move forward.'

'That's bull. We can't let outsiders start telling us what to do – we'd lose all our authority. They're from the Finance Department mate – the enemy. And, by the way, I'm having a real battle with them over my expenses. The deadline – written down in the procedure – has always been the 24th and they now tell me they've changed it to the 22nd and I'll have to wait a month. They can't go around changing the rules just like that!'

AUDITING

An audit is basically simple. If an audit is to be really useful it must be an exercise to learn from, for future development, rather than just a historic view of past activity. As a process, an audit means comparing what is with what ought to be, to identify any areas that need further investigation. It's what you do about the further investigation that makes the difference. In this chapter we are looking at an audit of the organisation's overall approach to health and safety, exploring its culture, behaviour and processes. An audit is a sort of health and safety medical, covering the whole corporate body, rather than a narrow investigation into any single organ or function. The results will be specific and unique to your organisation, given that all organisations are different in their nature and culture.

This means, for example, that while there are similarities in the processes of an organisational audit and some specific health and safety procedures such as risk assessment, the principal difference is that the health and safety audit is looking at the infrastructure and culture of a unique organisation as a foundation for every aspect of its health and safety development. Risk assessment, on the other hand, is one of the specific activities required of all managers, with rules and clear processes that can be specified and followed pretty consistently in any organisation, whatever its culture and infrastructure.

What auditing means

The word itself comes from a Latin root that is linked to the word for listening – audio is another derivation – and that's what auditors traditionally did. They listened, as the person whose actions were being reviewed explained what had happened, why and how. Then the auditor judged whether the actions were in line with standard practice or were out of order.

Most of us are familiar with auditing in its financial context, where the image is of someone independent checking the figures and the financial actions taken, to make sure they all make sense and are in line with acceptable procedures. In organisations that have to have their accounts audited by a qualified outsider, the acceptable procedures derive mainly from company law and to an extent from ethical business practice. In other words, there are set standards that the auditor uses, against which to measure what has been done and assess whether it is legal.

In health and safety, standards are set and requirements imposed at the legal level that can be used in an audit. If it were restricted to that specific area, the audit could be conducted using hard facts, clear requirements and a simple checklist derived from what the law says. However, start looking at behaviour and culture, and you leave clear-cut law behind you and enter the realm of blurred edges and the need to define for yourself what is appropriate. There is no clear definition of what is right when it comes to culture and behaviour, just a need to identify what is appropriate in the specific circumstances of this organisation. Therefore, you will have to design your own standards – and update them as circumstances change – using your own managerial judgement and your investigative and analytical skills.

In other words, auditing is a process of identifying what ought to be happening and comparing it with what is happening. Taken out of the financial context, anything can be audited, including:

- the extent to which your human resources match your requirements now and for the foreseeable future, in terms of number of people, their skills, qualifications, attitude, location and so on
- how well you meet occupational standards, like the Management Charter Initiative criteria that set out what makes a competent manager, or organisational standards like Investors in People
- the amount of output you have available from the machinery and equipment at your disposal, relative to the output requirements you have to meet
- the extent to which your health and safety policies, procedures, practices and culture are appropriate to truly effective operation.

However, the financial parallel is worth pursuing just a bit further. In the same way that we started by looking at auditors in the financial context, so we can look at how the results of a review of past and current activity can be used.

Historical information and the future

Published accounts must be a record of payments, purchases and actions that have been completed, or they can't be published as a matter of fact. One use of these accounts (once they're audited) is to prepare balance sheets, profit and loss accounts and annual reports. The information is used historically. It shows what has happened as a sort of snapshot over a past period.

In management accounting the emphasis is different. The information is used to inform future plans and actions, as managers plan ahead and use it to help make sensible decisions and realistic forecasts.

In health and safety this distinction relates to the different perspectives we have stressed throughout. The historical information is useful if it satisfies an inspector, or shows that the organisation and its managers have done what they should – but to be really worthwhile it has to do more than that. It should provide a starting point for improvement and development. Identifying what does and has happened and comparing it with what ought to happen makes active management of health and safety a real and exciting possibility.

In this chapter, you are going to be an auditor, not only listening but also looking, so that you can assess whether what happens now in terms of health and safety measures up to the standards that it should. You will see that in health and safety the audit is part of a process, where the results provide you with invaluable information on the gap between what does and should happen, and where development and change are needed as the first steps in a journey of continuous improvement.

HEALTH AND SAFETY AND CONTINUOUS IMPROVEMENT

Continuous improvement is a quality issue we've mentioned before, one that is central to best practice in quality management. Put simply, it says that everything can and should be improved all the time, not just once. This makes sense in the health and safety context because the target keeps shifting, whenever new factors come into the equation – factors like new laws and regulations that move the goal posts, staff changes that alter the status quo, and new equipment and materials that require specific and safe ways of working.

It also makes sense because making anything perfect is more of a goal then a practicality. The aim must be to become better and safer all the time, to enhance practices and attitudes and to make improvements based on what is learnt from audits, mistakes and incidents. But achieving perfection is always just out of reach, especially for the most health and safety conscious organisations which believe that, by definition, there is always room for improvement.

There are some clear steps in the continuous improvement process:

- identify what is required
- check what is happening in reality
- specify the gaps
- plan and take the action needed to fill the gaps
- review what is required and start the process again.

Unless an organisation is already committed to continuous improvement, in quality, operations, customer care and health and safety as just a few examples, the cycle has to start somewhere. In most situations, the most appropriate place is at the top of the diagram in Figure 3.1 (Specify what should be happening) through to the bottom right (Identify the differences). That's what this chapter concentrates on, as a way of getting started. The final point in the list makes it a never-ending cycle, where it tells you to go back to the top of the list and begin again, looking at what has changed and where you could tighten things up still further.

Auditing is essentially a reviewing activity, to help you establish the first two stages in the cycle – where you ought to be and where you are. From this you can put together the information at the third stage – the gaps that need to be tackled.

By the end of the book, when we have looked at a range of other issues that may need improvement, you should be in a position to plan and take the action needed. But it is important not to try and do everything at once. Changing and developing culture is a long-term process – a marathon rather than a sprint – so jumping into panic action, without thinking through the whole scenario properly, can lead to the wrong action, or one that doesn't stick. In any improvement that requires some degree of cultural change, it is essential to tackle the culture and the behaviour rather than go for quick fixes. So, this diagram comes up again later with some minor refinements, when you reach the point where taking action is the right thing to do.

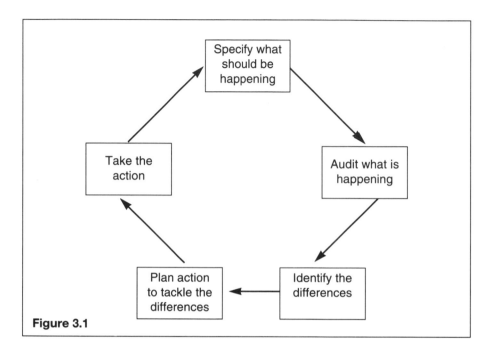

Figure 3.1

THREE AREAS IN AN ORGANISATIONAL SAFETY AUDIT

If an audit compares what happens with best practice, the starting point is to be clear about what best practice is. It's obvious that unless you know what you are aiming for, any checking you do will be meaningless. There are three issues to think about as you prepare a list of the characteristics and actions you wish to see in place – a sort of specification of what should be happening. These are:

- the importance of the culture set by top managers on the following two points; this is very difficult indeed to define in hard and fast terms

- the behaviour of people in carrying out policies, practices and procedures, and whether the behaviour fits with the statements; this is not easy to measure, as it is a softer, more fuzzy area and therefore more difficult to specify

- the measurable and visible statements about sound health and safety practice; these can be specified in detail.

We'll look at the background of each one, in turn, before moving on to specify what ought to be happening in your organisation and then reviewing it.

Culture is softest and hardest

The culture of an organisation determines the feel of the place, the way that people treat each other, the degree to which managers and other employees co-operate or compete. It sets the tone for how much inter-departmental rivalry and mistrust there is, or alternatively how well people operate across functional, departmental and hierarchical boundaries. It underpins the decision-making processes, the amount of involvement and empowerment that front line workers have in their own destiny, and so on.

Because it is a set of underlying values, beliefs and behaviours, it's difficult to apply a hard and fast specification to culture. What is clear is that the majority of people will adopt as their approach what they see being demonstrated by senior people as appropriate behaviour. If good practice and leadership by example are demonstrated from the top and across departmental boundaries, you're on to a winner. If not, you have problems, because the opposite side of the coin is that the cultural pressure will always win if there is any mismatch between how the organisation really is, and what it says in its slogans and pronouncements.

Give any group of employees a mission statement that says the organisation cares immensely about them and a manager who patently doesn't, and which one will they believe? It's not hard to figure out. Autocratic managers who operate by telling their people what to do, rather than by leading by example and encouraging everyone else to share in the process of making improvements, work against a positive health and safety culture.

Any attempt they suddenly make to open up major issues to consultation, involvement and joint problem-solving will be regarded with deep suspicion. It's simply out of character, and people will look for hidden motives ... 'where's the catch?'

Investors in People – a consultant's story (Part 1)

I work as an Investors in People consultant. The Investors in People approach to training and development requires the organisation to prove that it meets the standard set down. The first step in the organisation's journey towards formal assessment is generally an internal audit carried out by an outside consultant like me, to assess current performance against the standard and identify what action is needed. The audit includes interviews with a random selection of staff, to check whether people on the front line confirm what the written policies and the top managers say.

The first part of the standard is that the organisation makes clear its commitment to people as its central and most valuable resource, and that it takes that commitment seriously in terms of the training and development provided.

For some organisations this is not a problem – they are doing it anyway and staff find no difficulty accepting it and confirming it to the consultant when it comes out explicitly through the Investors in People process.

However, more often than not, when an organisation says to its employees that it values them, is determined to put in place systems and resources that ensure they are properly trained, the response is not 100% enthusiasm. It is more likely that the consultant hears comments like:

- pull the other one
- I've heard it all before
- they're lying to you
- not in this place!

This cynicism is an almost universal response from employees, when an organisation that they feel is autocratic and managed top-down, suddenly says it is working to different values and beliefs. Very few people will be surprised at this, and most will recognise the situation from their own experience. What the staff are saying is that the culture of this place is not one where people are valued, or are given appropriate consideration when it comes to training. Their view is based on the evidence of their own experience over previous years, and it isn't going to change overnight just because the managers who yesterday were acting like Attila the Boss are today trying to send out soft and caring messages. The message is seen as some sort of clever propaganda slogan rather than a statement to be trusted and believed.

One common way of demonstrating this relationship between real culture and the superficial slogans and symbols is to see the whole thing as an iceberg.

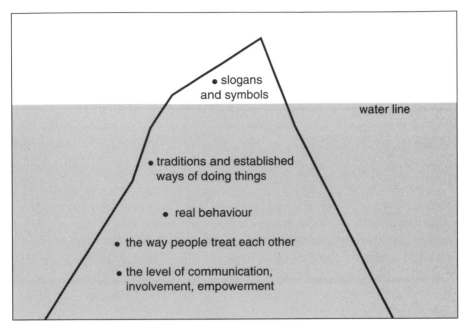

Figure 3.2

Only 10% of the iceberg is visible above the water, and it represents the visible parts of the organisation's values and beliefs – its slogans and all the good words that come down from above. The slogans can be words or symbols – statements about policies and beliefs, mission statements, posters, or mugs with smily faces, or a special promotion where the children are welcomed by a clown and given balloons and other goodies. You know the sort of thing, either from your own organisation or from places you visit, maybe as a customer. For instance, you walk into a retail outlet and see on the wall a poster that proclaims:

THIS ORGANISATION BELIEVES PASSIONATELY IN PEOPLE – AND BELIEVES THE CUSTOMER IS FAR AND AWAY THE MOST IMPORTANT PERSON HERE TODAY.

Unfortunately, the behaviour behind the scenes that the customer doesn't see – the way the people inside the organisation actually treat each other – doesn't operate like this. Managers rule by threat and it is made clear to sales staff that they are there to help the company first and the customers second. Sales are to be made at all costs, payment is on the basis of commission on sales and how many extended guarantees a sales assistant can screw out of customers, and there's an attitude of, 'If you don't like working here, there are plenty who would like it'.

Think about it ...

All you have to do to appreciate the real culture of such an organisation is to put yourself in the shoes of someone going off to work there in the morning and feel what it's like. How would you really operate at work – with an image of the customer as the most important person in your life, or as another punter to whom you might be able to sell something – anything?

The net result of this is that the poster about customer care is not only a waste of time – it's downright wrong. The staff see it as a lie or a con-trick, because they know what really happens, and the behaviour that you as a customer experience reflects the real culture that exists. You probably wait while you're ignored in favour of someone who looks as if they're going to spend more than you, and you are likely to be treated in a fairly off-hand way. You'll generally receive service that is less than welcoming. This is because the 90% of the iceberg determines where the visible 10% ends up – not the other way round.

The iceberg and health and safety

The visible 10% of the iceberg represents the publicly communicated face of an organisation's approach to health and safety. It's all the fine messages it sends out, all the posters it puts up, all the training events (however ineffective) it runs. This public part ranges from signs like *Please take a 10 minute break every half an hour from the VDU* and *Hard hats must be worn* to slogans *Your welfare is our concern* and health and safety policy statements.

> **Think about it ...**
>
> *What public health and safety messages does your organisation put out, to make up the visible 10%? How close are the reality of what is expected and the visible 10%?*

The 90% below the water line reflects the way things really are, the things people do, their real view of how important health and safety is in this organisation. And it's this that determines how they behave. If the 10% and the 90% are aligned with each other, and the messages are a real reflection of practice and commitment that goes on invisibly, then feel free to hold a small celebration – as long as it's all positive.

Unfortunately, all too often what is above the water line and what's below it are not only not the same – they are completely different and sometimes diametrically opposed. So, either management and/or staff say one thing but do another. Take the following case study.

3

Take our word for it ...

We've got a health and safety policy at work. It's mentioned in all the company literature and they're very proud of it. Indeed, we regularly send people off training. It's a joke, though. If you walk round the office you will see something quite different to all the slogans you see up. For a start, there are signs everywhere telling you never to prop open fire doors – but they're all propped open all the time. The amusing thing is, they're propped open with fire extinguishers in most places. In the finance department there are electrical leads all over the place because the computers haven't been properly set up. You could trip over them dead easy.

What's more, although the company says it values health and safety, when one of my people asked for a new back-friendly chair because he'd had a slipped disc, he was told there wasn't enough money in the budget and he would have to wait for another six months to get it. Funny, though, the boss got a new desk. The problem you see here is that they say one thing but we all know they don't really believe it. Is it any wonder then that you get people here doing things like propping open the fire doors with those fire extinguishers? They've even started rewriting some of the notices – changing letters and words so they make people laugh. That's how much of a joke it is.

This raises a central issue in the pursuit of a positive culture. The two big enemies when trying to establish a positive health and safety culture are these.

- People see it as someone else's job, or something that they don't need to bother with. A manager who role models the 'us and them' school of management is strengthening the enemy's hand.

- The level of action devoted to health and safety is pitched at the bare minimum needed to comply with the law.

Developing a positive health and safety culture means working to shift the culture that already exists. And as culture reflects established behaviour … the only place to start is with behaviour, the behaviour of managers. Staff will follow, but won't take a greater role in developing enhanced health and safety procedures and practices until and unless evidence has been produced that proves to their satisfaction that managers really do value people and their contribution to health and safety. Always remember this key point:

> *The only way to change culture is by changing behaviour.*

If a consultant turns up at your door and says they can change the culture of your organisation and the attitudes of your staff, quiz them on how they're going to do it. If they maintain that it's about slogans, mission statements and the visible 10%, probe very deeply and don't make a commitment until and unless you're convinced that the behaviour change that results will make a new culture emerge and stick. There are hundreds of examples of management employing an outside consultant to implement a new approach to quality, customer care or health and safety, in the mistaken belief that they (managers) can sit back and leave it all to a third party. It has never worked, it does not work now and it never will, although it can be an excellent way of spending large amounts of the company's cash.

We'll get you to examine the culture of your organisation in a bit more detail, after we've looked at the other areas that need measuring.

The soft parts are harder

Behaviour and attitudes that reflect the culture and are brought to the organisation by the individuals who work there are complex and difficult to measure. However, while it is not easy to check in a mathematical way, behaviour is at least visible so it's easier to check than attitude and is also easier to specify.

The sort of behaviour you can see is the way people respond to and carry out the policies and procedures with which they are issued. One difficulty facing many managers is that they are provided with policies and procedures and expected to make them work immediately. It is as if the expectation and belief of the people who devise the procedure is that simply printing the words on a piece of paper means the problem is solved, and that everyone will conform instantly. This is patently absurd, as the example in the section on culture, above, illustrates. The fact that you have a policy or a procedure doesn't mean it is working or that everybody follows it. In fact, even a law doesn't necessarily make it work – just think about the Community Charge and what happened there.

3

Think about it ...

Think about any aspect of the work you manage where there is a health and safety procedure that should always be adhered to. Now reflect on just how carefully everyone follows it all the time.

Or, think about a policy that an organisation you know has in place – maybe for health and safety, or equal opportunities, or another human resources area. Did the practice always match the policy to the letter?

In the experience of most managers there is a gap somewhere between policy and procedures and what happens on the ground. Take an apparently simple health and safety issue, for instance, and get a mental picture of what happens when there is no pressure on. Then compare this situation with one when there is a rush job, or a staff shortage. In the first situation the chances are that a great deal is said about working safely, not taking risks, wearing the right clothing and so on.

But some pressure from above, or a link between personal bonuses and the amount produced, can cause the good practice to go right out of the window. Results – output and outcomes – become paramount and everyone's approach seems to be that the ends justify the means.

Corners get cut, rules and regulations disregarded and normal behaviour increasingly is seen as that which is required under pressure. Good practice is just some set of words and documents that have no real impact on everyday life. And, of course, as you know, this becomes part of the organisation's culture – 'the way we do things round here'. Normal behaviour and attitudes (and normal does not necessarily mean right) set the tone for the way everything is tackled.

So, while anyone can devise and publish a document they call a health and safety procedure, making it work in practice is another problem altogether. It requires a specification of the behaviour neeeded to implement the policy and procedures consistently. But specifying behaviour is hard, and specifying attitudes is virtually a waste of time. You can't tell people what to think ... or rather, you can, but at best it's a waste of breath and at worst it's counter-productive. And this is a fundamental point of organisation culture.

Behaviour change has to come before attitude change. Telling people that they must be more health and safety conscious is point-less. The only way forward is to demonstrate that health and safety really does matter, and help them come to the conclusion for them-selves.

Investors in People – a consultant's story (Part 2)

I heard this sort of comment (e.g. pull the other one, I've heard it all before, they're lying to you, not in *this* place!) almost universally in a fabric works in the North West, when they started the Investors in People process eighteen months ago. It wasn't a surprising reaction really, because there was already a mission statement that said that staff were highly valued and treated with respect and consideration ... which they felt they weren't. I told the management team what they faced, but they said they really were prepared to see it through and not just pay lip service to it, so we drew up an action plan and worked on the processes.

One exercise they needed to carry out was some form of training needs appraisal interview of all staff, by their respective supervisors and line managers. The management team's first thought was to issue an instruc-tion that all managers and supervisors were to complete this within three weeks, to carry out the exercise sensitively, with respect and concern for all staff ... and return the required forms in triplicate. I mean to say! I managed to get them to hold back and think about the huge dangers here. If it went wrong at this stage the whole cause would be lost.

We gave the exercise a great deal longer, we looked at training people, raising their real awareness of what was happening and why, and we started the exercise top down, with senior managers going first. We made sure everyone knew this was the order things were happening in and we answered their questions as openly and honestly as we could.

The resistance was less than it might have been, because of the lead from the top, and as time went on we educated and trained all managers and supervisors in interviewing to identify their staff's training needs, and they conducted these interviews in a way that gave them and their teams a very positive experience. Then the managers made sure their people received the training they had agreed they needed and wanted, and the comments started to change.

The acceptance that it was a serious exercise was grudging at first, people were still sceptical as you might expect, but enthusiasm is catching and over the eighteen months the whole place started to buzz. To cut a long story short, the end result was that last week the external assessor went in, examined what happens (and interviewed staff) and they awarded them Investors in People status.

3

This success was not immediate, and it came only through personal example and commitment from the top and by the behaviour of the organisation as it reinforced its beliefs and values. The organisation had to put its money where its mouth was or nobody would have believed it. The staff's attitude change followed the change in behaviour.

Take a different example. Think about people's attitudes to sex discrimination in an organisation that has 300 employees and a clear anti-discrimination policy. It is an absolutely safe bet that within the 300 people there will be a number who are totally committed to the policy, a number who feel that all this 'feminist' stuff is over the top and wrong, and the majority who are somewhere in the middle. Naturally, if the organisation makes a lot of its values on equality, it will hope to attract staff with the same sort of general view, but it can't be guaranteed.

Education and persuasion through evidence and logic will always be important, but the bottom line is that no manager will succeed in changing overnight the personal beliefs of someone who naturally would discriminate, however much they counsel, preach or put forward a logical case. In some cases they couldn't change those beliefs given a lifetime – especially if all they do is talk. What they can do – as long as the organisation's behaviour is consistently backing up the policy – is to demonstrate behaviour that conforms to requirements, and require the same behaviour from other people.

The difficulty is that values and beliefs show through in attitude, in body language and other uncontrollable areas of behaviour, so getting people to behave appropriately is not always easy. But when it does happen there is then the prospect of attitudes changing gradually over time, as people see for themselves that the policy works.

Remember, the organisation's real culture and the expectations it has of how people must operate have to be in harmony. If the culture does not reinforce the policy in action, the culture will win out and the perception that discrimination is acceptable and normal will become even more deeply entrenched. Replace Investors in People and equal opportunities with health and safety and exactly the same principles about culture and behaviour float through.

Health and safety behaviour

The behaviour you need in health and safety is at three levels:

- policies and procedures that encourage people to take them seriously and behave appropriately
- compliance with the policies, procedures and safe systems of work
- an active and creative approach to identifying and removing real and potential problems.

The first of these is down to the policy-makers. The second can, to an extent, be forced, through instructions, orders and even making non-compliance a disciplinary issue. The third is different. It requires more of a cultural lead, with empowerment, openness and involvement of staff at all levels if they are going to make a real contribution.

The hard parts are easiest

The easiest of the three is the area of hard, measurable and visible aspects that any organisation has to cover to satisfy the law. Remember, there are some general issues that apply to all enterprises, and some other specific pieces of legislation that relate to certain industries. You always need to make sure that you are up to date and have covered both the general and the specific in your own circumstances.

The reason this is the easiest area is that it is factual and virtually a straight 'yes/no' review.

The relationship between health and safety culture, policy and practice

None of these aspects stands alone. For example, on the point of a health and safety policy, the first question is 'have we got one'. If you have you can tick the box and move on. But in terms of quality, what should a policy be like?

If it's worth doing, it's worth doing well. An effective policy is worth having, while one that doesn't work in practice is a waste of time and space. There's nothing very revolutionary about this, of course, but look at the health and safety policy in some organisations and it's a meaningless jumble of words with no practical application. The only reason there is a policy at all is that the law says there has to be, so they copy one from another organisation or give it to someone relatively junior to cobble together.

A sound policy must set high expectations and encourage people to believe that it can be achieved.

BUILDING THE HEALTH AND SAFETY SPECIFICATION

Having examined the three areas to be audited and specified, the next step is to prepare the specification against which to conduct the audit.

There are two main sources from which you can draw information towards your specification:

- external sources
- the organisation itself.

External sources

Much of the picture you need to build up can come only from your own organisation's context and circumstances. However, there is no point in reinventing the wheel, so it can be extremely productive to obtain outside and/or expert advice, help or example.

Statutory bodies and advice

The Health and Safety Executive has a vested interest in helping you develop a positive approach in your organisation. You may feel that its only interest is in policing the law and trying to catch you out – a little like one of the manager's views of auditors in the conversation that opened the chapter. Disabuse yourself of this misconception immediately.

We guarantee that you will be very pleasantly surprised at the reaction you get if you ring your local HSE, explain your intentions and ask them what support and help they can provide. Naturally, their involvement depends on their existing workload to an extent, and nobody can promise they will drop everything and rush round like a knight in shining armour. However, they will be keen to visit and help you, and will at the very least be able to send you several free leaflets and booklets, and recommend some other inexpensive reading that will provide you with a very sound starting point.

Benchmarking examples

This process – again often linked to quality management – is about identifying what can be achieved and examining how it has been achieved elsewhere. You can benchmark against other departments in your organisation, other branches and sites, or other organisations.

It avoids complacency and it opens up possibilities that might otherwise go unnoticed.

Boots and saddles

A safety officer in a manufacturing plant making parts and accessories for cycles was finding it hard to get employees, especially young employees, to wear the correct steel-capped footwear in certain parts of the factory. She knew she had to improve things, for legal reasons and also because of the potential human suffering and the financial costs of neglect.

She set herself an objective of doubling the current low level of use and, even though this only represented about 75% coverage of all staff all the time, she just about managed it through a process of carrot and stick. The carrot was an education and training scheme to bring home the personal benefits to employees and their feet if they conformed, and the stick was a campaign to make it a disciplinary offence not to wear the right clothing. Naturally, she felt pleased with her success and felt she had made a major difference.

At a health and safety conference she found herself talking to her counterpart in another industry and she talked proudly about her success. Soon, though, her pride was dented, as he told her that he had now achieved 94% success. He explained he had experienced the same problem and had followed the same route, with similar results.

However, he had then met the representative of a new and small firm making safety clothing, who had shown him some fashionable safety boots designed to look very much like the sort of boots that many young employees wore socially. They were more expensive to buy than the others, so he did some preliminary research. He worked out a slightly devious strategy, which meant showing them to the most recalcitrant workers, who were also seen as key influences amongst their peers on the shop floor. Where they led, others tended to follow. He very casually put the boots down on the table when he joined his 'targets' in a tea break, and when someone asked about them said it was a pity the firm couldn't buy these. Naturally, as not all staff would wear safety boots anyway it would be a waste of money … wouldn't it?

They had bitten, and almost demanded the boots. He reckoned that the way staff had started using them with virtually no work on his part meant that there had actually been a cost saving as a result of his reduced work on the problem, as well as the desired increase in use.

Sensibly, the first health and safety officer tried this out for herself, with very similar results.

What happened was that the first officer had been jolted out of a slightly complacent attitude by discovering how much better someone else could do. Sensibly, she had adopted and adapted their approach to suit her own situation and enjoyed further success.

The underlying lesson, though, is that even the 94% success level may be exceeded somewhere else. The danger remains that she might lapse back into complacency at 94% and stop trying to improve. It is not enough to rely on bumping into someone and them volunteering to tell you how well they're doing. Managing improvement is an active and not an accidental process.

Benchmarking is about identifying best practice elsewhere and then following it up, to identify new and higher standards of what is possible and to pick out what could be applicable from others' experience to your situation.

Think about it ...

What benchmarks could you identify in other departments, sites or organisations? Is there a situation or an individual which could give you ideas on what really could be achieved and how? The chances are there is, even if in the past you have just looked at this success and felt envious, or said it's all right for them. There is nothing to stop you setting out to find out more from them.

It may feel like cheating sometimes, because it means identifying how other people have got there, adopting their ideas insofar as they can be applied to your situation, and learning from their mistakes. A better way of seeing it is as common sense. There are no prizes for taking the hard route and going over ground you could avoid if you did some basic research.

Internal sources

Here you are examining what is required in your own organisational circumstances, which mostly means exploring for yourself.

Do we have ...

Starting with the factual issues, we can say that if the law specifies certain procedures and practices then you can construct virtually a 'yes/no' checklist. You started to look at this when you worked on the quiz in 'Health and safety matters', as part of the *basic principles* in the last chapter.

For example, a specification of what ought to be happening could be built around the following questions, amongst others.

- Do we have a health and safety policy?
- Do we display the required posters?
- Do we have employers' liability insurance?
- Do we have procedures for informing HSE appropriately of all accidents and work-related illnesses?
- Do we carry out risk assessments in all areas and record the results?

At some stage you need to construct a list for yourself, so you may want to take some time out now and draw up some ideas for that part of the specification while it's in your mind.

Specifying behaviour

There are three levels here:

1 the status of policies and procedures
2 the actual behaviour of people implementing safe systems of work
3 the extent to which people take the initiative in working actively to improve health and safety, rather than merely reacting to and complying with other people's instructions.

Each successive level depends on its predecessor, so if the audit shows that the first point is not being covered satisfactorily in the workplace, it is virtually impossible to work on the others.

1 The status of policies and procedures
Determining the required behaviour means first going behind the policies and procedures and specifying what has to happen to breathe life into what are otherwise just paper systems. For instance, if you have a health and safety policy, it means building a specification with questions like:

- does everyone get a copy – and do they believe it
- is it up to date, relevant and updated appropriately
- is it explained
- is it used in everyday work
- are its principles demonstrated in the daily actions of the organisation and its managers?

In other words, having a policy is one thing, but what impact does it have, how is it viewed by managers and other staff and how is it used?

So, if your policy was drawn up several years ago, is out of date but still gets trotted out unchanged to successive generations of new employees, you may as well not have one. Sure, you may be able to use it to get the organisation over the legal hurdle, but it's like having a forged MOT certificate for a car with no brakes.

2 Implementing safe systems and procedures

Specific procedures and systems are another example. The law says that you must devise and use safe systems of work, but these are the very systems that can be ditched when the pressure is on to complete that rush job, or complete a large order for a new customer. The questions you could use here are similar to those you would ask about the policy:

- is the safe system current and relevant
- are people trained in applying it
- is it industry best practice
- is it followed consistently and without fail
- when is it most likely to fail?

3 An active or reactive approach

What is under scrutiny here are the attitudes amongst people and the hard evidence of any meetings, discussions or other methods of encouraging and facilitating the active involvement of all staff in developing improvements to health and safety.

Much of the evidence can be collected through observation, so the specification could include criteria against which you can check, such as:

- the extent to which people have to be forced or instructed, for example, to follow procedures or wear the right clothing; or at the other extreme, the extent to which they do these things automatically
- the cleanliness and tidiness of the workplace; this is to an extent a tangible measure of good housekeeping, a simple but important element in maintaining a safe working environment

- what comes up as agenda items at staff meetings – whether health and safety is always or frequently there, in a prominent place on the agenda; look too at how it's handled – is it just an address from the person calling the meeting, or is there discussion, debate and involvement?

- if there are processes like suggestion schemes, improvement groups or team briefing sessions that include health and safety as a specific issue.

There is also the option to include in the specification some sort of attitude survey, where you ask people in all parts of the organisation and at all levels some simple and telling questions, like:

- who is responsible for health and safety

- what health and safety training do you get

- how important do you think health and safety is around here?

Identifying an appropriate culture

This is not so easy to quantify without a framework. There are several standard works on the culture of organisations that can help you sort out one of a range of models, but in the health and safety context we are most concerned with the extent to which management either tries to control everybody and everything, or empowers, trusts and supports people in their efforts to take a greater share of responsibility for their own work, their own quality and their own health and safety.

Your audit needs to identify which of these two cultures you work in, so you know more about what sort of task you face in trying to unlock a more active approach to health and safety across the entire workforce.

Broadly, some characteristics of the two reflect the work of Douglas McGregor, when he investigated management style in the 1960s and wrote about what he termed Theory X and Theory Y managers. He researched different beliefs among managers, about the way that other people behave, and identified that some managers (which he called Theory X) believe that:

- people dislike work and will avoid it if they possibly can

- the only way to get people to work is by exercising a high level of control and direction, issuing detailed orders and threatening punishment if people fail to carry them out

- this style of management is welcomed by most people, because they have little ambition, minimal commitment, no desire to take on responsibility and a big need for the security that comes from following someone else's instructions.

Theory Y managers, on the other hand, believe that people:

- do not inherently dislike work and, given the right conditions, want and need it to be a satisfying experience
- will manage themselves quite capably if they are given goals, objectives and targets that are realistic, challenging and achievable
- not only like taking responsibility but, given the opportunity, will actively look for it
- are under-developed in most organisations, that treat them as if they have the characteristics attributed to them by Theory X managers.

Remember, the categories McGregor used described what managers felt about people in general, and his point was that these inherent beliefs influence strongly the way that managers treat people. His focus was motivation at work, but given that you know the way people are treated is one of the cornerstones of culture, you can see how important the relationship is between the two areas of study. His work was on the style of individual managers, and we have simply gone one step further by saying that whole organisations often tend to demonstrate tendencies towards one or other of McGregor's sets of characteristics.

Appropriate rather than right

There is an important point about culture that has to be made. There is no single 'right' culture. For example, if you look at an appropriate culture for, say, the Samaritans, you would not come up with a heavily top-down, authoritarian style. It needs to be open, listening, responsive and caring, between workers as much as with clients, because the culture will always show through. On the other hand, if you were to define a culture that suited, say, a branch of the armed services, it would have none of the things that the Samaritans need. It would need to be characterised by rank being everything, orders having to be obeyed without question and there being no room for front line soldiers to question officers' orders as they go over the top.

However, in this book we are advocating clearly that a Theory Y approach in an organisation is more aligned to a positive approach to health and safety culture than is Theory X. There are exceptions, but it is generally appropriate to every organisation wanting to improve its approach to health and safety. You will recognise clear links between this view and the bits of Chapter 1 where we looked at the need for people to see some benefit for themselves before they undertake extra effort or a change in approach. Just telling people to do something does not gain compliance, let alone commitment, except in organisations like the army where the culture has to support a disciplined and quasi-legal approach.

The point is that most organisations – fire service, police and army and other similar examples aside – do not come under the heading of 'disciplined services'. That is to say that their culture does not, by definition, need to be authoritarian and run on top-down orders and instructions. Granted, there have to be rules and regulations in any organisation, but today's successful enterprises are most often those that treat people as if they had a brain and set out to unlock the talent that exists in the workforce.

Developing the health and safety culture is about raising the level of commitment and involvement in all parts of the organisation, and at all levels. Therefore, our contention that Theory Y is generally more appropriate is based on the belief that most organisations would benefit if they were to examine their culture and move towards a situation where staff were empowered to take responsibility and help make the decisions that shape the organisation. Read any of the leading management writers – Peters, Waterman, Handy, Rosabeth Moss Kanter to name just a few – and you will see the same message coming through consistently, borne out by example after example.

Drawing the specification together

Having explored the background to the three areas to be audited – culture, behaviour and the concrete issues – and looked at the key questions around which your specification of an ideal situation can be devised, the next step is to structure the framework of criteria for the audit.

There is no single matrix of acceptable health and safety performance that can fit all organisations and their needs, you must devise your own specification for acceptable and appropriate performance. It will need to cover both hard and soft aspects and will have to be something that you can use as a measuring tool.

For some areas that you audit it will be simple enough to draw up a yes/no option. But for the others something more sophisticated is required. Don't worry – the secret is to keep it as simple as possible and to allow yourself the right to be subjective. Doing anything is infinitely better than doing nothing. The point is that if the best available measure is a personal assessment … then that's the best you can do. Just because there is no hard and neutral set of criteria does not mean you should not do the best you can, even if it feels as if you're working in a way that is a bit like judging ice skating, where some things get marks for technical accuracy against clear criteria while others are about a subjective view of artistic interpretation. The latter may be an inexact science, but it still gets assessed.

The only rule of thumb is that you should always try and find the most objective or measurable factors you can, even if they are still fairly subjective.

CARRYING OUT THE AUDIT

It should now be possible to compare what is happening with the specification you have drawn up to indicate what you feel should be happening. Make sure you have established for yourself what you want to see in place before you start assessing current performance.

Some clues on how to do it

All you now need to do is to review what is happening, in terms of culture, behaviour and day to day practice, against your specification. However, it can feel rather daunting to be faced with an exercise that you not only have to carry out, but also have to design. Perhaps a few ideas on how to go about it might be helpful.

What is your culture like?

Having an outline description of an appropriate culture gives you a benchmark against which to assess the culture as it really is. You can assess your culture in any way you like. Here are a few possibilities.

1 Get a group of people together, show them an outline of two or more different cultures, and ask them to debate and brainstorm which one is closest to that applying in the organisation; make sure people can back up their opinions with examples and facts.

2 Brainstorm it yourself, by just writing down off the top of your head all the examples of organisational behaviour you can think of and then collating the results to give you a general picture.

3 Do the brainstorm in (2) above, but do it under some headings, to break it down into bite-size chunks, maybe headings like, involvement, delegation, support from above, open communication, and so on.

4 Use one of the many standard and detailed inventories that help you assess organisation culture. Your personnel manager or someone in training and development will know where to help you locate one, or you could refer to a book like *Gods of Management*, by Charles Handy.

However, as a starter we have devised a simple questionnaire that you should find helpful. It focuses on the two types of culture that are reflected in McGregor's Theory X and Theory Y management, which are described a little earlier in the chapter.

Have a go at the following inventory to help you identify broadly which of these two cultures you work in. It is short and simple and all you have to do is look at the twelve statements on the left and decide how true it is of your organisation. If, on balance, it's more true than untrue, tick the 'true' box. If not, tick the 'untrue' box.

Senior and middle managers in my organisation:	*True*	*Untrue*
Ignore or play down ideas that come up from below, because they weren't invented at the top and they challenge the status of senior people	☐	☐
Work in a highly-structured hierarchy that ensures any ideas or proposals from front line workers and supervisors get filtered out at several layers of management	☐	☐
Wait a while, then re-invent the ideas that came from below and claim them as the creative products of top managers	☐	☐
Believe that people are motivated by fear and criticism rather than praise and support	☐	☐
See suggestions for improvement as personal criticism and, rather than listening to the real point and making any changes, spend time justifying and strengthening the present position	☐	☐
Value rules and regulations more than creativity and ideas, and judge people's worth by how well they keep their nose clean and never raise difficult issues	☐	☐
Plan and implement change in secret and present it to the people who are directly affected, as a fait accompli – it stops them feeling too secure and gives management the edge	☐	☐
Believe that most people only come to work for the money and would rip the firm off given half a chance, so their ideas must have an ulterior motive that will harm the organisation	☐	☐
Assume that only managers really know anything worth knowing, with the more senior managers knowing most and junior employees having no right to opinions	☐	☐
Dislike and avoid delegation of any parts of their own role, and always insist on checking (or even doing) the work of the people who report to them	☐	☐

	True	*Untrue*
Believe that information and knowledge is power, and hold back as much as they can from the people working below them, because otherwise they'd know as much as managers	☐	☐
See other departments, functions and management levels as the enemy, preferring to try and score points off them and blame them rather than work together as part of one team	☐	☐

You've probably worked out that, the more ticks you had in the 'true' column, the harder it is going to be to develop a culture that really supports and develops a positive approach to active health and safety management. It doesn't make it impossible, but if control and power are held tightly at the top of a status-conscious structure, the potential for making any real inroads into the values and beliefs that set the operational tone is reduced.

The bottom line is that you cannot expect people to behave and operate in what you think is an appropriate manner, if the 'way we do things round here' and the example of those making the rules is at odds with your expectations. The culture is developed by people's behaviour, by the establishment of norms that become the accepted way of working.

This means that when you come to identify the gaps that have to be worked on, any changes to the management style which reinforces and feeds the culture are going to come high on the list of priorities.

How is the behaviour?

The specification here should allow you to check behaviour fairly closely. But behaviour is not easy, so these are some ideas on how to do it.

- Observe the process for yourself, from the outside, and set out a scale for the whole issue, say by giving marks out of 10.
- Involve a sample of people in a survey, using simple questionnaires and synthesising the results to increase the chances of getting a statistically sound result.

- Do your own observation and ask others to do the same using the same criteria. Then compare your results with theirs.
- Prepare an interview checklist and ask a sample of people for their views, in an internal market research survey.
- Either using your own judgement or working with a group, break down big processes, problems and issues into smaller components, so you can look at each one separately and with more accuracy.

Checking the factual aspects

It is relatively easy to assess this against a checklist built around a series of 'yes/no' options. The results will give you hard information on how to make accurate judgements about what needs to be tackled just to stay in line with the legal requirements.

Identifying the gaps

Reviewing each of the three areas against the criteria you set is like a simple sum. Take x from y and you're left with z. Y is the situation you want to see, X is what is happening at the moment, and Z are the gaps.

PLANNING SOME ACTION

The action plan here focuses on drawing up the specification and the review process to identify the gaps on which you need to work. If you decide to follow it through you should end up with a workable approach that will enable you to conduct a meaningful audit.

Action Plan

In order to draw up a specification for each of the three areas I need to:

1 Do the following things:

(*A few examples might include: list the documents we must have, clarify the criteria that make them effective and not just bits of paper in a file, identify what safe systems of work are in place, obtain copies of them, check what legal requirements there are*)

2 Talk to/involve/obtain information from the following people:

The processes I intend to use to assess current performance are:

1 For the concrete and measurable aspects:

2 For the behavioural issues:

3 For the culture:

Playing your part in health and safety

Two colleagues were having a drink at the end of a day's managing.

'What do you really think about the way we handle health and safety – I mean, really?'

'No problem. I look after myself because I know nobody else is going to bother. All the bumf comes down to me from up the line and I send back the right memos – and I set the tone for all my people … it's my department.'

'But the people in your department don't do what they ought to, do they – be honest. They lark about with the equipment, they never tidy up the work area and they draw moustaches on the posters!'

'Now hang on a minute – you've only been here a few months and you may not know the ropes yet, but anyone in this place who goes at it like a bull at a gate is never going to get anywhere. I put the posters up, I send them off on courses and I look after my own office. The rest is up to them.'

'But your office is a tip! What sort of example is that? You even had a fire the other week, when your waste paper bin was too close to the electric heater. All right, it was put out quickly, but it was a joke. You're even known as 'firebrand' now.'

'You've got it wrong. I control my own work space and I leave everyone else to control theirs. What I do in my office is my business. They don't tell me what to do and I leave them alone. They'll sort their own office out for themselves – it's obvious because they'll only hurt themselves if they don't.'

'But it isn't everyone for themselves – it's a joint responsibility, surely? What you do in your office has a direct impact on anyone who dares to go through the door – especially if they might get engulfed in flames.'

'Oh, give it a rest. You'll see the light in the end – just give it time. Anyway, 'scuse me a minute – I want to complain to the manager. There's a really slippery floor in the gents and they obviously haven't told the cleaner that someone could hurt themselves.'

HEALTH AND SAFETY CULTURE AND PEOPLE

At the heart of a positive health and safety culture is the idea that everyone has a role to play and a stake in making their organisation safer and healthier. This is vital as it helps get away from the idea that effective health and safety can simply be imposed from above, left to someone else or just bought in.

Responsibility for developing the culture is not the same as legal responsibility, although there are parallels. For example, one parallel is that managers hold a greater share of responsibility in each case, and in setting and changing culture it's the top-down demonstration of different behaviour that starts to chip away at how everyone else does things. The top-down example of a new approach leads everyone else to see that this is the right and acceptable way of doing things in this organisation. But, as you know from the last chapter, it isn't a quick or easy job. It's more a marathon than a sprint – but even the marathon starts somewhere.

To change culture, first change behaviour

Remember, the word 'culture' is used to encapsulate *the way we do things round here*. It's shorthand for the way that the organisation feels as a place to be, for the way its values and beliefs show through in its decision-making and communication processes, for the way people at all levels value and respect each other – or don't – and the way every action that takes place tells you something about the nature of the organisational beast.

However, it is important to stress that while everyone has a role, not everyone has the same responsibilities. The actual responsibility for keeping the whole organisation healthy and safe falls fairly and squarely on senior managers and it is their actions and the actions of managers right down the line which create the culture, ideally one where everyone plays a constructive part.

So it isn't just the top managers – it's everyone. The cascade effect works its way through the part that all these groups have to play:

- senior managers
- middle managers
- front-line managers
- other staff.

SENIOR MANAGERS

Senior managers have a whole range of rules and responsibilities in establishing a health and safety culture, which can be divided into two basic areas:

- tangibles
- intangibles.

The ability to lead and guide is crucial to both areas, as is the need to set a framework that is effective and well-supported both financially and in terms of time and other resources.

Although the health and safety culture idea stresses the importance of teamwork, involvement and ownership across the organisation, very little of any real worth will happen without the active involvement and genuine commitment of senior managers. This is an issue that we stressed in Chapter 1, where it was made clear that it's foolish to expect people to change their values and beliefs just because someone says they ought to. They change their stance because of the benefits, and whether these are altruistic, or wanting to look like a really nice person, or wanting to reduce potential costs doesn't matter in the slightest.

However, it would be an almost impossible situation if you were not at least somewhere near the top management level and were fighting battles against senior management where you worked. So remember how important it is to plan strategically to raise their commitment, based on issues that you know matter to them.

The tangible things

Senior managers are policy makers, so they have a responsibility for making sure an effective health and safety policy is in place. If they don't do it, nobody else can.

Of course, as we have already seen, ultimately senior managers are legally responsible for health and safety in any organisation. It is their job to safeguard the health and safety of people working in the organisation. The following are some of the practical and tangible things senior managers should be doing in order to establish a health and safety culture:

- coming up with a **health and safety policy** that is clearly thought through
- putting a strategy in place to implement the policy and then integrating it into the general business activity of the company.

Integrating health and safety into the heart of the business

It's all too easy to come up with a policy that sounds great but isn't clearly thought through and doesn't fit in with the whole organisation. One of the essential ideas of health and safety culture is that health and safety should become part of the everyday working of an organisation. It shouldn't be an extra or a luxury or the part that always suffers when times are busy or hard.

It should become like clockwork and seem as natural as any other part of the business. Indeed, it should be seen as a crucial part of the business of the organisation – it should be part of the annual business plan. It is impossible to be committed to quality, for instance, without having a health and safety policy and a strategy to implement it.

It's up to senior managers to make sure that it's given due priority and is properly integrated into the general business activity of the company.

Some ways this can be done are set out in the following checklist. Let's look at some of these in a bit more detail.

Some ways of giving health and safety due priority:

- give overall co-ordinating responsibility to someone senior, whose other management role is at the heart of corporate planning – someone on the management team, for example
- put in place a structure for planning, implementing, reviewing and auditing the health and safety policy

---

- introduce a structure for turning policy into strategic plans

- put in place a strategy for developing and reviewing health and safety targets

- encourage senior managers to take individual responsibility for health and safety – use a carrot not a stick

- build it into the accountabilities in managers' job descriptions, so it turns up each year as a measurable activity during appraisal

- make it number one agenda item at all company meetings and not part of any other business or the last item

- fund adequate publicity for health and safety.

Let's look at some of these in a bit more detail.

4

Structures

Policy, strategy and plans will only emerge if they are part of the normal business of the organisation. Building a structure that specifies what sort of policy is needed, who is involved in devising/reviewing/amending it and what criteria are to be used by whom, when, to measure success, is the only way to put and keep the policy approach on the company's agenda. If it isn't planned specifically with dates and names, it won't happen. Planning and specifying that this will happen is in the hands of senior managers. Only they can make it happen consistently across the organisation, with any clear sense of purpose.

Once the policy is clear, a structure for middle managers to devise and implement strategies to deliver it is the essential next step. This might involve all managers having to produce departmental plans regularly each year, that clearly mesh with the overall corporate policy and plan. It happens in most organisations with budgets and/or training needs and/or human resource planning, so it's a short step from there to health and safety – if the process works, use it again.

The strategies should have, as a central component, objectives or targets that specify what is to be achieved, by when – and the targets must be measurable.

Targets

If you don't know where you're going, you can't plan to get there, which is why you must have targets. And if you do, it's essential that you can measure your progress and assess when you've made it, or there is no focus and no sustainable drive or energy behind the action. Wanting to do better is fine, but how much better – 4%, 8%, 29%?

If you can measure something, you need systems for doing the measurement. Measuring how well you're doing is the only way to know whether you're on course, you can stay on course, or need to change course.

Targets also give you a handle on whether the policy is successful. Without some hard information that can go to the policy makers, how can they tell whether it is working, or is simply words on a piece of paper.

Clarifying individual managers' responsibility

Giving overall responsibility to a senior generic manager raises the profile straight away. It is a simple alternative to another common practice – looking round and seeing which mug we can dump health and safety on. Often, by the way, it's the personnel department, which in many organisations is still outside the main line management structure and there as a central resource unit, without any direct clout or real say in corporate policy.

This can be an excellent tactic if you are trying to change the way a management team thinks of health and safety. The chances are that at least one person in that team really does care about health and safety – and unless you're a management team member yourself, they inevitably have more clout than you do. So identify yourself as an ally, work with them and support them as they work on their colleagues.

You also need to find some way of raising the profile of health and safety so middle and junior managers want to take it seriously, rather than feel they have to pretend they are. Having a lead at management team level is an excellent start, and some organisations give cash and other rewards to managers who make most progress in health and safety. Or they put in every manager's job description an accountability that goes a lot further than the usual trite comment at the bottom of the document. Once it is in the accountabilities, it is simple to start setting individual targets with managers at annual appraisal meetings, so they automatically focus on the issues on which they know they will be assessed next time.

Simply asking questions and giving feedback can strengthen the position. Try sending people who work for you a one-line note every seven days, asking what improvements to health and safety they have made this week, and praising them when they come up with examples.

Monitoring and reviewing

Part of this is to do with being committed to monitoring accidents, near misses and ill-health incidents and seeing if a pattern emerges that can then be tackled and addressed.

Another part is about the targets and the policy, and monitoring progress constantly. Reviews look back, so regular review meetings provide a strong and clear focus for managers and others on what has happened, and what needs to happen next.

In all these actions, senior managers have to recognise they are putting in place long-term structures and procedures for health and safety and not simply a quick fix. The health and safety culture is based on continuity and gradual improvement and senior managers need to create the strategic climate where longer-term planning can take place. The culture shifts as behaviour shifts, so it has to be seen as a steady march forward.

Investigating some other senior management issues

There is a whole range of issues around these specific tasks and actions that senior managers also need to address, if they are going to provide the conditions that ensure they will work. You will recognise all of them.

Putting your money where your mouth is

For instance, it's no good saying that more attention must be paid to health and safety if there are inadequate resources to do the job. There would be no point in saying that you are interested in a health and safety culture and then not providing any time or money for training – it would simply reinforce the disparity between the visible part of the culture iceberg and the 90% under the water.

However, sometimes there is an answer even in apparently impossible situations. It can come from a review of where resources go now. Most organisations have a training budget and a health and safety budget. The trick may be to switch the priorities and put the limited resources to use differently, rather than keep spending on things that don't always work, and complaining that there is no extra cash available.

Auditing for continuous improvement

Another key responsibility of senior managers in this tangible area is to set up some form of health and safety audit. Any successful health and safety policy has to be linked to clear auditing of procedures, products and outputs. Its only when you know and can check what is happening that you are able to make real improvements.

The credibility factor

Throughout the book you will see involvement at all levels stressed as a crucial factor in developing culture, and the need for managers to demonstrate best practice. This means that you have to have credibility, or you will be seen as someone who knows all the right words, but not the real tune. The chances are that many people all the way down the organisation know a lot about health and safety, and if you start talking nonsense or make a real gaffe, then your one chance of establishing a credible presence has gone.

Twenty questions – a senior management credibility checklist

The following checklist should help you answer some of the questions you need to address as a manager. See if you spot any gaps or problems you need to tackle.

1 Are you clear on your legal obligations for health and safety?

2 Who are the safety representatives?

3 Do you know what all the relevant current legislation says?

4 Where could you get good health and safety advice?

5 What health and safety training has taken place in the organisation in the past year? What specifically was it for?

6 What would you do at the moment if an accident occurred?

7 What auditing procedures have you got in place?

8   How does the company record health and safety incidents?

9   What issues have been raised as potential problems in the past year? By whom? Why?

10 How do you track trends in health and safety in the company?

11 Have there been any planned improvements in the last year?

12 How much do you spend on health and safety?

13 Where might you need to focus spending this year?

14 Does the annual business review include health and safety?

15 With whom do you deal in HSE or the local authority?

16 Do you have a health and safety committee and who is on it?

17 What is the organisation's health and safety policy?

18 Who keeps records of risk assessments?

19 What are the major health and safety risks in your industry?

4

20 How many people have been off work in the organisation for more than three days as a result of a work-related problem in the past year?

21 What system is used to get information on new legislation and regulations circulated to the right people?

These questions will help you to think through whether you have coherently worked out your obligations and responsibilities as a policy maker in an organisation. They also make the world of difference to your credibility, and therefore to the speed and ease with which you can make a real impact.

Co-ordinating procedures

One of the things that needs doing in this tangible area by a senior manager is either putting together or co-ordinating the production of a set of health and safety statements and written procedures. Any organisation committed to a health and safety culture needs a set of written procedures for health and safety.

There is a legal and a cultural basis for this. The legal background is that the organisation has to implement safe systems of work. These are designed and put in place to ensure that the safe way of doing something is the way it is done, every time. One way of reinfᵒrcing these is through written procedures. It's not the only way, of course – training and coaching are other approaches that also reinforce the use of safe systems.

The cultural side is that procedures need to be realistic and reflect the world as it is, or they will be at odds with the real culture. They have to represent safe systems where relevant, of course, and they should also be shared widely. Wherever possible procedures should be developed in conjunction and consultation with the staff who have to carry them out.

Check the documentation

Check back in your files to see if you have:

- written statements of general health and safety policy and strategic objectives

- written statements about planning, measuring, reviewing and auditing

- written statements about how to implement policy and strategy

- general plans containing specific objectives for each year.

Put all these things together and you should have come up with a range of tangible things that could help health and safety flourish at work. Any gaps mean you know where attention needs to be paid.

It's these tangible things that act as the kind of skeleton or backbone of any health and safety culture. They're always there for guidance and to help steer you through any rough times. They're also physical evidence of the organisation's interest and commitment and, while they are not enough on their own, they are a solid foundation. Building on the foundation is about buttressing the written words with personal communication and demonstrations of behaviour – issues you'll see covered in Chapter 6.

The intangible things

But as well as these very tangible and useful things you should be putting in place, there is a whole range of intangible areas that you need to deal with as a senior manager. After all you could develop a first-class set of policies and frameworks, but still not get staff involved. In this case the written material is fine but there is no actual health and safety culture.

The key word here is **leadership**, especially leading by example. Leadership is not just about charismatic senior people, making others want to follow them blindly. It is about leading from the middle, working with the team and supporting and guiding.

> *Leadership is ... a creative process in itself and is about helping the people around you to be more creative too; [leadership] depends on teams and teamwork; the effective leader is a coach, helping his or her people to perform at their best.*
>
> How To Lead a Winning Team,
> Morris S., Knasel E. and Willcocks G. Pitman Publishing 1995

It's important to show that you really are serious about health and safety – especially if you found in the past that attempts to raise the health and safety profile got off to a false start. People need to be able to see that you have a visible and genuine commitment to health and safety and are able to give the lead.

There is likely to be a lot of debate and even cynicism about health and safety if you start to launch a health and safety culture. You'll probably hear people saying that they haven't got time to do it properly or it's a distraction from the real work of the business or that they have heard it all before and that you are not serious. This means that you will probably have to start fighting the corner for health and safety and showing that you really value it, and indeed you will have to show why you value it.

A large part of this leadership business is to show enthusiasm for your health and safety culture. This may well mean making yourself available on the shop floor, in the offices, and being able to answer questions when asked. Sometimes the questions will depend on the sorts of information covered in the credibility checklist, but at other times they will require you to be enthusiastic and to communicate a genuine image of commitment yourself. If you don't really believe it

… don't say it. Your body language will always tell others very clearly just how committed you really are.

Another intangible area of leadership is having vision and demonstrating values. It's the vision thing that will help people understand why you are taking health and safety seriously, and how they fit into the vision.

This is how one chief executive at an NHS trust describes the way that he uses his leadership vision.

Down amongst the bedpans

We wanted to make sure that the environment in a hospital was really healthy and safe for staff. This sounds a bit funny but hospitals are actually quite dangerous places to work. For instance, we've a lot of manual handling type back injuries. Nurses and other staff often have to lift patients, and if they haven't been properly trained or don't carry out what they have learned in practice, we do get a lot of back injuries.

We launched a new initiative to get people to take health and safety a bit more seriously. We had a slogan and I went round the different wards and departments explaining why we thought it was important. I did meet quite a lot of hostility and negative attitudes, but the important thing was to show that we were serious.

I decided that I would start working one shift a week just so that I could get closer to the people doing the work and spread the message. I used to call this my 'down amongst the bed-pans' session. I'd work in a ward and I would do anything – change the sheets, anything at all really. I could then observe and talk to people about health and safety and help really get the message through – and show that we were committed to it. I'm sure that it's showing this enthusiasm and vision that allowed everyone to see that we were serious. It also gave them a senior person they could come and talk to and ask questions. People came up to me and said they wanted training in various areas and I was able to assure them that there was the budget and tell them the route they had to go through to get their training.

Of course we backed all this up with a set of policies and an effective audit system that allowed us to develop those tangible areas too.

I was also able to start rewarding good performance. We used to give out a little reward for improved health and safety every month and I was the person who presented this. It might sound odd but some of the people who received it said it was the first time they had ever actually seen me about the hospital, let alone met me. So this very visible leadership was absolutely crucial.

Chief Executive, NHS Trust.

MIDDLE MANAGERS

Managers in the middle have got an absolutely crucial role in a health and safety culture.

On the one hand they need to interpret messages and statements that come from senior managers and make them real and tangible to staff. They have also got a coaching and development role – acting as health and safety role model.

The following are just some of the different roles that middle managers can adopt to help a health and safety culture survive and thrive.

The role model

One of the important things that middle managers can do is to be a role model for staff. Middle managers can demonstrate how to work in a healthy and safe way and act as standard bearers for the change to better work practices. So it is important to demonstrate constantly healthy and safe ways of working. It helps counter any negative attitudes and works against examples of dangerous practices.

Acting as a role model could include:

- running impromptu and other training sessions
- praising good performance when you see it.

Praise is a very important weapon in bringing about any change. It's very important that people think you are sincere and that you are behind the initiative.

All too often, thoroughly good campaigns to increase health and safety launched by senior managers run aground on the cynicism of the manager in the middle.

It's very important that you are able to show that you are absolutely behind the move to a health and safety culture and that you take plenty of time to explain to people within your team and department why it's so important.

The snow plough

Another crucial area for middle managers is providing the means for health and safety to happen. If you are perpetually squeezing health and safety then it will suffer, like any other area of work that has to produce too much from too few resources.

So the snow plough middle manager, knowing the importance of the issues and recognising the long-term benefits of taking early action, will:

- allocate time; for on-the-job and off-the-job training for instance
- identify the need for and sources of money and make the case for a budget for health and safety
- recognise the need for other resources.

The snow plough middle manager will not get deflected from their health and safety vision by tight deadlines. Equally, they will fight for resources for their own staff, so they can make improvements and generate ideas and solutions to health and safety problems.

Working through others

We had this problem with health and safety. We had a couple of accidents with fork-lift trucks in the warehouse. I gave the drivers a rollicking and then came in all weekend on my own trying to work out a solution.

Bleary-eyed on Monday I called my supervisors together and told them I had solved the problem. There was a silence and one of them said, 'Sorry Alastair, but that won't work'. Jim then told me of his own plan. It was much better than mine and required us to alter the traffic flow within the warehouse and issue new guidelines and get the training end sorted out. I then went to the company accountant and got the money for Jim to make the system work in practice. It wasn't easy – I had to make a sound case out, but I kept at it and in the end she recognised I knew what I was talking about, meant what I was saying, and was only asking for something that was common sense.

I learned that you have to work through others – through their ideas and enthusiasms and not just try to push everything through yourself.

Alastair Whitson, middle manager

The target setter

Middle managers have the ability to set targets for their team for improving health and safety.

Health and safety can feel very abstract if it isn't set to firm targets – remember the impact of the words at the start of Chapter 2. Part of the reason for setting targets is to allow people to start feeling ownership and commitment to the idea of health and safety. It introduces a sense of urgency too. No-one wants to miss one of their targets.

Without targets the temptation is to drift along. If you can start setting sensible and realistic health and safety targets you can then move things on and use the targets to help people develop. If your teams, or individuals within them, miss targets then the wrong approach is to shout and bawl at them. First it gets their backs up, and second, you may not have given them the skills, knowledge and understanding needed to cope with what was required. Instead, use the targets to work with them and to identify what help they need if they are to meet them in the future. This links in nicely with the coaching role of middle managers.

The coach

4

Coaching for health and safety is one of the crucial roles middle managers can perform. At the heart of the coaching role is the brief to help and support your staff to learn and always look for opportunities to help them develop their role.

The coaching manager always looks to help his or her staff do more than they are doing at present. In health and safety terms, this means looking to develop their awareness of the issues and take on more responsibility for identifying risks.

Taking the coaching approach

The following is an extract from *Successful Empowerment in a Week* by Steve Morris and Graham Willcocks (Hodder and Stoughton, London 1995). Although written in a slightly different context the relevance to health and safety is obvious.

The coach is someone who:
- can bring out the best in the individuals they manage
- encourages staff to develop skills and abilities by giving them new experiences and challenges

- always looks for talents and helps to develop these amongst their people.

Coaches:
- set challenging goals and targets for their people
- are tolerant of their people's mistakes and learning
- give plenty of praise
- encourage their people
- are excellent listeners
- are patient.

Coaches may use any of the following ways of using and developing their people's talents.
- Job rotation or job shadowing within the team so people can see and/or experience other roles and jobs.
- Push to get people on training courses they feel would benefit them.
- Put a team member forward for a prestige project team.
- Give a team member a chance to attend a company social event.
- Give your people a chance to go out and meet suppliers or sub-contractors.
- Give individuals a chance to chair a meeting.

The final six points are all possible ways of increasing staff's knowledge of health and safety issues.

The message carrier

Central to the health and safety culture is the idea that everyone has suggestions to make on health and safety improvements. Indeed, the closer to the work you get, the more relevant and realistic the ideas are likely to be. This is because the people who do the work are most likely to have insights into the work itself and the dangers involved. All too often ideas have come down from senior managers which haven't been realistic and so haven't been taken up.

As a middle manager one of your roles is to help your people – by giving them the space, time and encouragement – to come up with ideas and improvements in health and safety. When you have got these ideas and suggestions for improvements the next job is to feed them back up the line to policy makers within the organisation.

As part of this you will need to fight for resources to make these ideas happen in the workplace. So the middle manager's role is to help people feel involved and empowered to play an active contribution to improving health and safety where they work.

The auditor

One of the things you will do is to carry out health and safety audits with your team – a topic you looked at in Chapter 3.

Because you are that much closer to the game than senior managers, you will be able to carry out an honest audit which builds on real and first-hand awareness of the realities of life within your department.

The translator

And finally an important role for middle managers is that of translator. Often health and safety messages come down from senior managers in a way that makes perfect sense to them but may seem very difficult for front line staff to action.

So one of the things you will be doing is helping to change and present the messages that come down from senior managers in a way that is easily understood by your people, so they can act on them. You will look at this in more detail in Chapter 6.

SUPERVISORS AND OTHER FRONT LINE MANAGERS

Front-line managers are just that – on the front-line; which makes them key players in establishing a health and safety culture. This is because front-line managers:

- are best placed to have a real insight into what happens in the workplace – where the dangers are and where people take short-cuts or ignore guidelines; they possess masses of up-to-date information about health and safety as it happens
- generally are close to and have the trust of their team, so can lead any move to a health and safety culture by example
- are likely to be able to generate plenty of ideas for improvement from their team.

The following are just some of the roles and actions front-line managers can take to make a health and safety culture work in practice.

Running a health and safety conscious induction

Front-line managers are in many ways responsible for communicating the values of an organisation. This is particularly important when new staff are being inducted. It is the front-line manager who is likely to give plenty of messages about 'the way we do things around here'.

If these messages are dismissive of, are cynical about or disregard health and safety the chances are that new employees will quickly take them to heart and act accordingly. A good, positive and rigorous induction conducted by a committed supervisor is a key way of establishing a health and safety culture.

Insisting on the right environment

The wrong environment often causes health and safety problems. Mess, dirt, grime and clutter all help cause accidents. Just think about the tangle of leads at the back of most computers and it's obvious that if they're not kept tidy they can cause slips, trips and falls.

The supervisor has a role to play in insisting that the work environment is safe and free from dangerous debris. Part of this may be that the supervisor needs to tackle middle and senior management for the resources or training to make the environment safer.

In an organisation where middle managers don't take health and safety seriously, front-line supervisors are in an almost impossible position. They represent the feelings of their team and have to convey concerns and problems upwards, if they are to do their job properly and keep their boss informed about issues that may disrupt output or productivity. They also have a legal duty to ensure that their team works in safe conditions, well maintained buildings and so on. But if they are told to get back to work and stop whining, they end up as piggy in the middle. Either they press the point and get marked as barrack-room lawyers by their boss, or they fail to press the point and are perceived by their team as someone who fails to work with and support them, failing to lead from the middle.

Making your contribution count

The following is based on a true story.

We had a supervisor where we work who one day came to her line manager with a health and safety concern. She registered her worry and said that something ought to be done before there was an accident.

She then left it at that. She continued to walk past the problem every day for the next six months. She didn't raise it again, she just ignored it. She felt she had done her bit.

Some time later there was an accident, just as she had predicted.

Clearly her middle manager was at fault for not following up the concern. But what frustrated me was that she felt she had done enough by mentioning the problem in passing on just one occasion.

I wanted her to feel ownership of the problem and to keep up the pressure. I wanted her to feel able to come to me if there was no action. I would have done something about it and we wouldn't have had an accident.

4

Front line managers need real support. It should come high on your list of priorities for action, in developing a positive culture.

Checking on performance

The supervisor is close to the work – very close. It is this closeness that allows the supervisor to check on health and safety standards and performance regularly and stringently.

The supervisor is there with their team and can monitor performance regularly. This information needs to be acted upon and passed up the line if there are wider health and safety implications.

Leading

The front-line manager, like other managers, needs to lead by example. Sloppy health and safety standards from the supervisor will quickly pass to the rest of the team.

Supervisors are at the vanguard of any change – they lead by example. You may simply need to show people how to work more safely and healthily, and train them on the job.

Generating information

As a front-line manager you are likely to get lots of health and safety information passing through your hands.

The key with any information is to decide what is relevant and what isn't, and then to make use of the important parts.

You need to pass on health and safety information in a way which is easily understood, and hand up the line any concerns about health and safety.

FRONT LINE STAFF

It's the front line staff who are often left out in any drive to improve health and safety. There is the wrong assumption that if you get people at the top behind health and safety, then the job's done – everything else will fall into place after that. In reality, unless front line staff are fully involved in the detail and the development of health and safety, then it stands an excellent chance of foundering.

One idea that is both practical and supportive of a better health and safety culture is that front line staff should form a team.

This means that you shouldn't only see health and safety in *your* area as a concern. Rather you should be looking for improvements in health and safety across your team, and looking out for your fellow colleagues. In other words, if you can improve health and safety in their work too, you won't just be doing them a favour, you'll be helping the whole team.

So, front line staff have a number of different roles. These include:

- reporting accidents honestly; all too often accidents and near misses happen and aren't reported – sometimes because people think they are too busy to report to them or feel they might get in trouble as a result

- looking for improvements; the people closest to the job are ideally placed to make recommendations for improvements in health and safety; they are likely to know what the dangerous equipment is, what the dangerous practice is, and what short-cuts people take in their daily work

- having a voice; it's no good seeing problems and then not saying anything.

Although ideally placed to spot health and safety problems and do the things listed above, these are not always easy for front line workers to do. What makes it especially hard for them is working in a culture where everything comes from above – information and instructions in particular. The outcome that is in everyone's interests is that all employees should be constantly vigilant about things that could cause harm or be unsafe.

In a positive health and safety culture this leads on to every accident and incident being reported promptly and honestly, with the person doing the reporting seen as someone helping solve a problem, not causing one. Report every accident or near miss honestly and in a way that can be useful in terms of looking for improvements.

PLANNING SOME ACTION

Start by asking yourself how well your senior, middle and front-line managers measure up to the roles described in this chapter, to get a clear picture.

4

ACTION PLAN

The positive aspects of how senior managers operate are:

The areas that need improvement are:

The positive aspects of how middle managers operate are:

The areas that need improvement are:

The positive aspects of how front line managers operate are:

The areas that need improvement are:

4

The positive aspects of how front line workers operate are:

The areas that need improvement are:

I believe I can make the following changes:

To achieve these changes I need to take the following action:

To take this action successfully I need help in the form of:

Assessing the risks

Two colleagues were having a drink at the end of a day's managing.

'How did you handle that memo that came round, saying we all had to carry out risk assessments in line with the HSE booklet? Shall we go for that table over there? Your shoelace is undone again by the way.'

5

'No problem. I just went round and listed all the possibilities I could think of. There are dozens, of course, but at least I've got them recorded now and sent it off, as we have to. (Excuse me, can I get through with these drinks, please? Thanks.) Bloody nuisance all this paperwork.'

'Yes, but it's not just paperwork is it? I mean, writing it down is only to record what you really did, once you've done it. It isn't the writing down that matters – it's the investigation. Your shoelace ...'

'When you've been around as long as I have you develop a sort of 'nose' for the risks, a sort of management sixth sense. I don't need to investigate things – I know what the risks are where I work and I control them pretty tightly, thank you very much! Come on, keep right behind me or we'll never get through.'

'Yes. OK. Well, I think it's a useful way of helping develop awareness amongst everyone, about simple things we can put right. I know you've got signs up saying "Beware. Frayed carpet!" and "Mind you don't trip over the electrical cables – it damages the equipment!" but it feels as if all that's happened is that everyone's got used to it that way.'

'As long as everyone knows what to watch out for it's not a problem. It's ... oh damn. Now look what you've made me do!'

'Sorry ... I trod on your shoelace. I did warn you.'

'Yes, but I knew about it and so did you. You should have been more careful. Now the drink's all over the floor.'

THERE'S ALWAYS THE RISK ...

Risk assessment is a legal requirement, but don't let that put you off. Don't ignore or give short change to one of the most positive and powerful processes in health and safety management that can:

- ensure you stay on the right side of the law
- reduce the chances of accidents and illnesses where you work
- involve other people in improving the safety of the workplace
- make a significant contribution to the behaviour change that is needed to drag culture change along behind it.

We certainly need to explore the fundamentals of risk assessment as a process, covering the first two of the bullet points above. However, we are exploring the detail of set processes as well as the context of organisation culture. Therefore it is important to extend the examination, and look at the major part that an active and serious approach to risk assessment plays in helping to develop and maintain a positive health and safety culture.

We'll start with the process.

THE RISK ASSESSMENT PROCESS

The aim of risk assessment is to put you in control of the risks inherent in the activity and the physical surroundings of your workplace, so you can ensure nobody is hurt or made ill by accidents and eventualities that could have been prevented. It is therefore completely in line with the benefits of a positive approach to health and safety that you have seen in earlier chapters.

Essentially, risk assessment is remarkably simple. It is an active process that involves taking the time to examine the workplace and find the things that could go wrong. Having found them, it follows that you need to make sure that every possible precaution is in place to stop the worst happening, and if it isn't, to take the necessary and appropriate steps.

Common sense figures throughout the process and some reassuring key issues to bear in mind are that it:

- should not clog up the system with trivial matters – to do so interferes with the need to address more serious and major issues

- is not a complex science – identifying hazards and risks is a matter of simple and practical action
- may well cost little or nothing to sort out a problem, while reducing the potential for you being hit with all the costs of an accident
- generally takes a few minutes and saves far more time than it takes.

How to do it

Basically, as long as you do it in a way that works for you, and it's one that fulfils the criteria, there is no prescribed way of carrying out risk assessment. To find out how many ways there were in operation, we asked a sample number of managers how they tackled it, reminding them gently that it is a requirement under the law. The answers we got included:

'Is it really a legal thing? I didn't know that.'

'This is a new office. There aren't any real risks here.'

'The health and safety officer covers all that side of things.'

'I give it to my deputy to do. It works for me that way.'

'I just walk round and look.'

'I walk round and have a look for myself, and we spend some time in team meetings gathering ideas and discussing it.'

'I daren't start – I know there's so much that needs doing, that I'd feel very exposed if I wrote it all down and couldn't do it all.'

Some of these are downright worrying, others give some cause for concern and only one really starts to capture the full potential of risk assessment as a tool for continuous improvement. Let's look at the statements in a bit more detail.

Is it really a legal requirement ... even in new offices?

Yes, it is a legal requirement. Assessing risks, taking appropriate action and recording what has been done is essential. It applies in every work situation and has to be recorded where an organisation has more than four employees. There are no exemptions, whether you're a service organisation, an office or even self-employed.

However, don't let the mistaken belief that it's a requirement – and maybe another one of those bureaucratic bits of nonsense – cloud your judgement and leave you wanting to opt out. It is such a cracking good approach to developing a positive culture that any manager who is not personally involved should feel a real sense of deprivation. It should be interesting, informative and extremely helpful to culture development if handled sensibly.

Someone else covers it

True, you don't have to do it yourself, and as long as someone competent is doing it regularly and correctly it's all right. But why not get involved yourself? It isn't hard and it's not something you can pass or fail.

Then there's the issue of what your behaviour tells other people about your commitment to health and safety. Their view is going to be that lack of involvement equals lack of interest, equals lack of real commitment.

Think about it ...

Someone else is reviewing your work area and your practices. Does this not have an effect on how seriously you treat any feedback they give you, and wouldn't you be more likely to make sensible decisions on what needs doing if you did the assessment yourself? Why don't you treat this management activity in the same way as you do others? Presumably you don't ask someone else to come in and tell you how many staff you need, or how to run your core operations, so why abdicate this crucial part of the work?

The bottom line is, what sort of personal commitment to health and safety does it demonstrate if you opt out of risk assessment and don't take the chance to work co-operatively with the rest of your team?

Even if you work in an organisation that nominates someone else to carry out all risk assessment, there's nothing to stop you getting involved and playing a central part ... except yourself and your view of the priority that health and safety is given. Not only does it increase your own knowledge and control over your own operations, the culture message it sends out to your people is entirely positive.

Walking about

Believe it or not, this is probably the best way of handling it. It is recommended by HSE as an approach that pays dividends. Naturally, if you can get the rest of your team to walk around as well you're going to pick up more information, through more pairs of eyes.

The single most effective approach to gathering information is as simple as that – walk around and involve other people in walking around as well. There are other strands of information that can help build up the full picture, as you will see, but walking around is a good start.

Finding so much it's impossible to know where to start

Fear of getting health and safety wrong can lead people to do nothing, on the basis that if we don't know about a problem the HSE can't get us for it. Well, actually they can, because you should be investigating so you do know about it, but in any event this is another area where the difference between your perception of authority and the real attitude of HSE might amaze you. Their line is that they appreciate you can't turn everything round overnight, so they don't expect it.

5

What they do expect is that managers make an effort to identify the areas of significant risk and sort out things that clearly need to be tackled as a priority. They also expect that you don't ignore risks just because you think they are low or medium, rather than high, but the bottom line is that you are expected, in their words:

> *… to do what is reasonably practicable to keep your workplace safe.*

In other words, as long as you do what you can, and it does the job and is practicable, you're on to a winner. The important thing is to make a start and tackle the priorities first. Once this is done, the behaviour change that it triggers tends to develop an impetus of its own, and the emphasis shifts from finding reasons for not doing something, to creating ways in which something can be done.

> *Think about it ...*
>
> *Bring to mind one of those health and safety problems you keep meaning to do something about – one that will take only a few minutes and very few, if any, resources to sort out once and for all.*
>
> *Sort it out, now. You will feel incredibly good about having achieved something positive, and probably quite surprised about how simple and painless it was to do it, instead of spending twice the time it took to sort out finding ways to avoid it.*

A SYSTEMATIC APPROACH TO RISK ASSESSMENT

By taking the risk assessment process apart and sorting it into six main stages, it becomes easy to understand, easy to manage and easy to do. The six key stages are:

1 **Looking at the workplace to identify hazards – the things that could go wrong and cause harm.**
2 **Work out who could be harmed and in what way if they did go wrong.**
3 **Work out the level of risk, by assessing the likelihood of it going wrong and the impact**
4 **Work to eliminate or reduce the risks where there is a significant or real chance of an accident or illness.**
5 **Record what you did.**
6 **Go back and start again.**

Let's look at each one in more depth. As we do, we'll add layers of detail stage by stage, to build a picture that increasingly enables you to take control of your own work environment.

Identify the hazards

Hazards and risks are not the same thing. A car parked on the pavement is a hazard to pedestrians, but it poses an infinitely greater risk to someone who is visually impaired. Most sighted people would notice it and walk round it. Hazards, therefore, are fairly neutral. They have the potential to cause harm, but can only be judged as a risk once the surrounding factors are known.

At this stage the job is to spot the hazards rather than analyse the risks. In the work environment this means coming up with answers to a simple question:

What could go wrong and cause harm?

You can use various sources of information to make your list.

Walking about with your eyes open

Listing all the hazards in your workplace is all there is to this first stage. However, to list hazards you first have to spot them and this can be deceptively tricky. The trouble is that the commonplace can become all too familiar, and blend into the surroundings.

In other words, a hazard you have lived with at work for years has by now faded into the background and lost its impact as a potential risk. It becomes part of the physical culture, the way things are done. Never sit at a desk and imagine another room or a different part of the work area – you'll miss the items you're most familiar with. Physically get up and walk about.

5

Think about it ...

What examples are there in your work environment of this problem? Windows that have to be propped open, electrical leads taped to the floor, machines that really need extra guards? Be honest – very few people can deny they know of one or two. Can you really put your hand on your heart and say there isn't a fire door wedged open somewhere?

Anyone doing this alone needs a degree of detachment to allow them to distance themselves from their own situation and see things through fresh eyes, as if they were coming to work for the first time and were looking for every possible problem. At all costs, the investigation must be factual and objective, listing everything and avoiding the temptation to explain away and justify why something is as it is.

Other people walking

Involving other people is really a much more powerful approach. The more eyes looking for hazards the better. There are several examples of how the involvement of others is used to ensure better coverage.

- In some organisations, managers work with each other either as partners or as teams, and drop in to have a look round someone else's work area. Because it is an agreed arrangement, the feedback is regarded as positive information on which to base a more detailed assessment. Sometimes, what one manager does not see as a hazard is viewed entirely differently by another, adding to the scope for action.

- Alternatively, some managers brief a complete outsider – maybe a personal friend – to come in, have a look round and report back.

- Teams are particularly powerful. One way of handling it that has been proved to work very well is to brief the team to walk around and list as many hazards as they can. Then, at a debriefing session, all the hazards are listed and a broad picture developed. In some places, they even run competitions and award a prize to whichever individual or small team can spot the most hazards. It's amazing how much a financial inducement or even a little friendly rivalry makes people stand back and look properly.

The documentary evidence

It can be particularly helpful to analyse records such as sickness, absence, accidents and incidents, to identify any patterns that otherwise get missed.

The ozone layer

A legal office in Bristol installed a second laser printer on a desk alongside a word processor. It was in a small office used by someone with the specialist job of producing contracts.

It was well used and everyone was pleased with the extra facility, until the office manager spotted that the individual who used the word processor and printer had gone home early several times with a headache. It might have been coincidence, but she went back to the printer manual and reread one of the pages that had been skipped in the excitement of getting it up and running. It said:

> *Ozone gas is emitted by almost all laser printers and photocopiers. Ozone can be an irritant and there are limits to the amount of exposure to ozone that anyone should experience (currently 0.1 parts ozone per million of air). This printer operates well below that level, but should be installed in a well ventilated area, especially if other copiers or printers are in the same location.*

There was no serious harm done, but the office manager had not noticed that hazard from a physical inspection. It came to light from recorded sickness and the manual that came with the printer.

Work out who could be harmed, and how

This shouldn't pose too much of a problem, except that it is another area where familiarity can lead one to forget certain individuals and groups. You can either think the situation through and identify anyone who could be harmed or, to ensure a consistent approach and that every angle is covered, draw up a standard checklist like the one that follows. It can be used in all hazard spotting in one particular factory, and simply lists all the people who could conceivably be harmed. It just needs to be ticked where appropriate, before making any further comment.

CHECKLIST OF PEOPLE POTENTIALLY AT RISK

The hazard in question is _____

_____

Those who could be harmed are:

	Tick for yes	*Number of people?*
• worker(s) involved in a specific task	☐	☐
• worker(s) in the immediate vicinity	☐	☐
• anyone who is beside/under/near the hazard in question	☐	☐
• people who are in the area outside normal hours (e.g. cleaning staff)	☐	☐
• outside contractors	☐	☐
• members of the public on site or in the vicinity	☐	☐
• purchasers or users of end products	☐	☐
• porters disposing of materials and substances	☐	☐
• contractors removing materials and substances from the premises	☐	☐
• other (specify)	☐	☐

For every one ticked, the way they could be harmed is through:

1 _____

2 _____

3 _____

4 _____

5 _____

6 _____

Work out the level of risk

A judgement is now needed on the degree of risk. This means balancing and weighing a number of factors. The checklist has provided data on who could be harmed and how many people could be involved, but you also have to consider questions like:

- how frequently are people at risk
- what is the likelihood of it going wrong
- how serious would the impact be?

The issue of judgement is where things start to get difficult to set out as a mathematical formula. There are no simple answers here, and your evaluation of the risk level depends every time on the balance between the various factors. For many managers this is a real blockage. The feeling that they have to get it absolutely right when it seems like a specialist job, puts many off starting or getting involved. However, it is crucial that every manager feels reassured by the fact that they are not expected to do more than their best. To quote the HSE leaflet, *5 Steps to Risk Assessment:*

5

> *Assessments need to be suitable and sufficient, not perfect.*

Different people will assess risk differently. There is likely to be quite a high correlation between their various findings, but there will be variations and that's OK. Using a form of factor analysis can help avoid making snap judgements, and develop a sharper focus on the real level of risk. For example, most people might say immediately that using a very dangerous chemical is a far greater risk than a tiny rip in a carpet.

But you may decide that the small rip in the carpet is a very high risk, that could trip up one or more of the hundreds of staff, visitors and members of the public who have to pass it daily.

On the other hand, you might feel that you are faced with a minor risk from the chemical, which is used only by qualified and trained staff in an enclosed and ventilated area once a month, following a safe system of work to the letter.

In another situation, the chemical could be a weed killer used weekly in public areas, while the rip in the carpet is by a desk in a private office and is not in a main pathway. The levels of risk change completely. In each case the hazard is constant, but what has changed is the number of people exposed to it, the chances of it going wrong and the seriousness of the impact.

Weighting the factors

One way of tackling the issue of risk levels is to assess each factor in the range separately. There are matrices available to help you draw up arithmetical models of risk level, or you can do a simple sum yourself.

However, if you do use an arithmetical approach, never rely on the figures. As the computer world has long said, garbage in, garbage out. If you are attributing figures to different factors then there is a human element involved. Only ever use the results of numerical risk analysis models as a prompt for further personal judgement or group debate.

For instance, you could work on a model using three factors, where for each factor you can attribute up to 5 points, 1 being insignificant and 5 being very significant. Having looked at each hazard against all the factors and reached a set of marks for each one, multiply them together and you get a total.

Example

Hazard 1 – a rip in the carpet by a desk in accounts

Who at risk: staff in the department
cleaners, 20 people in total, only one at a time   Factor 3

Likelihood of incident   Factor 5

Seriousness potential   Factor 4

                                                          3 x 5 x 4 = 45

Hazard 2 – use of isocyanate paint

Who at risk: paint sprayers (3)   Factor 3

Likelihood of incident   Factor 1

Seriousness potential   Factor 5

                                                          3 x 1 x 5 = 15

> **Think about it ...**
>
> *How can the use of a substance known to be damaging to health –*
> *two-pack isocyanate paint – be a third of the risk of a rip in someone's*
> *carpet?*

The reasons are broadly reflected in the factor weightings. The manager doing the assessment identified that there were no measures in place to control the hazard from the ripped carpet. Someone was going to fall, the only questions were when and how seriously. Possibly it wouldn't be that serious although the figure given is one person's estimate and their decision was to look towards a worst case scenario. The degree of likelihood and the fact that all sorts of people were exposed to it made it a relatively high priority.

The paint sprayers, on the other hand, were trained to use the materials, had breathing apparatus and showers and worked in a ventilated booth with an efficient extractor system. If the extractor system failed or the door was opened, the spraying equipment cut out automatically, so no-one else was at risk. Granted, the effects of an incident would be potentially very serious, but the other factors reduced the overall score considerably.

The point is though, that if the scores were discussed by a group of people in the team, they might see it differently and add information to the arguments. The scores themselves are not necessarily right, but they are a starting point that can trigger informed debate.

Work on the risks

Having identified all the hazards and categorised them in some way so they can be judged as low, medium or high risks (or your own priority classification), it is essential to evaluate the measures in place to remove and reduce the risk.

In the last chapter we looked at auditing. It's the same sort of process. If we take the paint spraying booths, the manager can claim, for example, that:

● the physical environment (sealed booth, extraction etc.) is the right specification

- personal equipment (breathing masks, coveralls etc.) is to industry standard
- safety precautions (cut-outs) are working and effective
- people are trained and competent
- a written safe system of work exists and is followed.

There isn't really anything else than can be, or needs to be done. The risk assessment shows there is a risk, but everything that needs to be done is being done. Any changes, of course, mean reviewing the situation and repeating the assessment.

On the ripped carpet this isn't the case. The rip must be fixed – and while that may mean putting some hazard warning tape over it immediately, this can only be a very temporary solution. There is a maxim that you can apply to sound health and safety, that comes across as a consistent message from HSE. It is that, except where protective equipment and clothing are appropriate in their own right, you don't issue them until you've worked on the basic problem. In other words, give people hard hats if their work requires it, but if the roof leaks then sort out the leak and don't just give everyone an umbrella.

Interestingly, it costs just a few pounds to make a phone call and get a professional in to sew up or seal a small rip in most carpets. Sorting out health and safety problems is not necessarily a time-consuming or an expensive business.

Record what you did

Keeping a record certainly covers the legal requirements, which include:

- possibly needing to show them at an inspection
- in the worst possible scenario, having a file to refer to if there is legal action by one of the staff member or a members of the public.

It also means you can refer back and track the history of any risk you have started to tackle before. You have to keep records of risk assessments if the organisation has five or more employees, even though you don't have to show how you did the assessment.

What you do need to show is that you made a proper check, that you tackled any hazard that posed a significant risk, that what is in place now has cut the risk to a low level, and that your actions were reasonable. You do need to show that your judgement about the significance of the risk took account of which and how many people could be harmed.

However, when you run repeat assessments there is no requirement that you have to repeat the same paperwork every time. It is essential that you can pull out documents that show that the risks have been assessed and tackled, but if existing reports do that – they'll do nicely. The format of the documents is up to the individual manager and the organisation, so it clearly isn't a massive bureaucratic paper chase.

There isn't anything particularly difficult or threatening about all that, really. Managers keep records of their actions in virtually all other activities, so recording your risk assessment activity is not going to make a massive difference.

Go back and start again

There would be no need to reassess if nothing changed. But most things have a habit of changing frequently and substantially these days. You are likely to encounter, in the course of a few months one or more of these and other changes:

5

● new staff

● new materials

● changes to the physical layout of the workplace

● different machinery or equipment

● new procedures, regulations or systems.

It is not necessary to start from scratch all over again, but any significant change may bring with it the need for a revision to the measures in place to limit risk. As has been stressed several times, it's common sense.

There is benefit in going back occasionally and checking, even if you don't think there has been a change. Sometimes change takes place slowly and quietly, tiny step by tiny step. This is exceptionally hard to spot and it can lead to a significant change taking place over time, that has not been apparent. It's like a minor drop in performance with your car. If it is very gradual the drop is unnoticeable day to day, but have it checked one year later and the total change becomes all too apparent.

On the other hand, there may have been no change and your last assessment will still be valid. That's no problem either – it's like an annual medical, where the result you want to hear is that your health is at least as good as it was last year.

The sum of the parts

It pays to think laterally a little, as well. It is virtually impossible for an accident to result from one single factor. For example, driving a car on a deserted motorway at night when you're not tired is a low risk. Add some fog, some rain, a couple of other drivers who are over-tired and the situation changes radically.

A complex machine at work may present a low level of risk when used in accordance with the safe working system, but add some horse-play between employees just after they have been paid, some materials clogging up the work area, employees back from the pub at lunch time, and you're in a different ball game.

One way of working on these multi-factor situations is to carry out some scenario planning. Ideally in a team, just ask the question *'what if ...'* about as many facets of the situation as you can come up with. Fire is a good example, because it requires three components to take place – heat, fuel and air.

Removing any one component removes the risk of a fire, so if you have a properly maintained electric heater at work, surrounded by air, it will not start a fire unless there is something that will smoulder and flame. However, put a stack of papers next to it and you have all three components present. So, a team might ask the following question:

What if the untidiness in the office spread to that corner and papers were placed against the heater?

Alternatively, the question can be asked another way looking back from a hypothetical problem:

What if there were a fire – what could have caused it?

Think about it ...

The one element that is present in all accidents is the human factor.

So although physics tells you that this fire is the result of heater, paper and air … really it's the person who put the paper there in the first place, and the manager who didn't stop it happening. This brings the issue right back to people, behaviour and culture. Any manager who handles risk assessment in an enthusiastic and committed way inevitably engenders a sense of enthusiasm and commitment in the rest of the team.

THE BRIDGE FROM RISK ASSESSMENT TO HEALTH AND SAFETY CULTURE

Imagine the difference in the impact of the following two scenarios.

Scenario 1

You work for someone who seems intent on keeping you down. You are aware of a risk from a worn power cable as it enters a machine housing, and one from a loose handrail on the stairs, and have reported them to the supervisor. But nothing is done about them. The health and safety officer carries out routine spot checks, but didn't have time to go upstairs, and missed the cable last time. You know that your supervisor will shout at you if you go back a second time.

You feel powerless to take any further steps, and are unwilling to go directly to the health and safety officer for fear of being victimised. Over coffee, you and the rest of the team catalogue all the hazards you know about, and make sure you at least keep each other informed about what risks to watch out for.

Scenario 2

Your supervisor calls you all together and says that, while she is responsible for health and safety generally in the area, she wants your help and involvement to identify and make improvements. The first thing she asks is whether you know of anything that needs attention, and you comment on your two issues. The cable is replaced by maintenance within the hour, but the handrail is not done. However, the supervisor comes back and says that it has been checked and, while it is loose, it is not coming away in the immediate future and will be dealt with in time.

The next step is that the supervisor asks you to walk around as if you were new, and see what else you can come up with.

5

Unless you are exceptional, the first scenario will lead you to avoid communication, assume that the supervisor has no commitment to your health and safety, and is generally not someone you like, respect or trust.

Initially you may be cynical in the second scenario, but you want to get the message across about the power cable, and the door is now wide open. Seeing the cable replaced tends to make you accept the explanation about the handrail. You are now involved – hooked – and when the call comes to find other hazards there's very little that would stop you. It really does feel like a partnership.

Empathy

The point of looking at the situation from the position of someone working for you is that it gives you an empathetic view. Empathy is not the same as sympathy – which is feeling sorry for someone. Empathy has been described as:

> *Putting yourself in someone else's shoes and feeling where they pinch.*

In other words, it means standing where they do and trying to experience their feelings and reactions. Interestingly, human beings are remarkably consistent in the way they react to being managed. If you feel better in a situation where the boss trusts you and gives you responsibility, rest assured others will too. The aim is to increase the level to which everyone in the organisation is taking an active part in improving the health and safety continuously – and that means involving them and getting their commitment level up through motivation.

McGregor's investigations into motivation and individuals' level of commitment, culminating in the Theory X and Theory Y descriptions, are supported by other investigations into what motivates people.

> **Think about it ...**
>
> *Are you more motivated to perform well by a salary raise and a bigger office, or by the chance to take increased responsibility, a greater level of creative work and generally increased job satisfaction?*

The vast majority of people are motivated more by the latter set of issues than the former – always given that they are being paid enough not to have worries about the mortgage or rent, and the food. More money is nice, but it doesn't generally produce a long-term increase in commitment. That comes from the job satisfaction end of the spectrum.

Hygiene factors and motivators

Frederick Herzberg was another investigator into motivation. His findings were that factors split into two broad groups, although they overlap in some places, as no two people are motivated by exactly the same set of issues. Incidentally, notice that we are not saying that you motivate your staff. This is because it is not possible. An individual's motivation comes from within – their manager can only provide a climate which helps it grow and develop, or squashes and flattens it.

Hygiene factors

Herzberg found that one set of factors – what he termed 'hygiene factors' had a potentially negative effect on motivation. By this he meant that if they were wrong they would block any attempts to get someone to improve their motivation and commitment. Too little salary to live on stops people feeling motivated – it just makes them worried and annoyed. So too do perceived unfairness – someone believing they have been overlooked for promotion, overtime or praise – and physical working conditions – temperature, room size, surroundings and so on.

Look at it this way. Someone in a room that is too small for comfort will not work properly. They moan about it, feel aggrieved and believe the organisation and the manager don't care about them. They get a room that's big enough and the problem is removed. Giving them a room that's bigger than they need doesn't keep increasing their motivation.

Or look at it this way. The hygiene factors are those things that an employee in a civilised society has a right to expect. It shouldn't be a bonus to get a decent place to work, or a living wage. Neither should it be treated as a special or unusual reward to work for a competent and fair boss. The point is that Herzberg discovered that the greatest blockage to commitment and motivation is unsatisfactory management. Unfair managers, who impose petty rules and restrictions, fail to communicate and see everyone working for them as cannon fodder. A little bit like the Theory X manager, maybe?

Motivators

On the other side of the equation, he found that positive motivators include responsibility, feedback and praise (when it's due), more interesting and creative work, the chance to see the results of one's efforts ... and all those job satisfaction issues. Very few people find this surprising – so why is it so unusual to find a consistent pattern of management that works in this way? Why do some individuals turn into Theory X zombies when they adopt the title 'manager'?

The lesson for health and safety is simple. The simple truth is that, if you want to manage health and safety better, you just have to manage better.

Better management

If management is getting results through other people – which is a fairly standard definition – then the emphasis in health and safety is to involve other people in their own health and safety destiny.

If any manager wants to raise the level of commitment to and motivation for health and safety, he or she needs to let go of the reins a bit and start believing that the workforce has a brain.

Think about it ...

How many people do you really know who come to work with the intention of getting it wrong, or going home unhappy?

How many people do you know who would prefer to put themselves at risk of injury or disease, given the choice and the real information and power needed to make that choice?

Nor do we. People will very rarely let you down if, for instance, you:

● trust them

● communicate with them properly and brief them clearly

- give them something worthwhile to do
- hand over responsibility for it to them
- support them in their endeavours
- give them constructive feedback on what they did well and where they can improve
- provide the opportunities for them to acquire the skills and knowledge they need to do more creative work
- let them see exactly what part they have played in the team's, the department's and the organisation's success.

They (and for 'they' could be substituted 'we' or 'you') will be motivated to take more responsibility for their own health and safety, if only you empower them to do so.

Risk assessment and culture

The links between a positive culture and an active approach to risk assessment that involves everyone should be pretty clear. Put simply, if you do it all for them, they will never own any part of it.

5

Think about it ...

You decide to change something simple at work – maybe the way desks or machines are arranged. You implement the change and you watch as everyone shakes their head and says it'll never work.

But your decision is exactly the same as the one they would have made, had they been asked. What's the difference? Yes, it's the fact that the first decision was someone else's and the second was theirs. Same physical change – totally different level of commitment to it.

Ownership of an issue is regarded by many as an overused term and concept, much beloved by management consultants. Unfortunately, it matters. Give people a stake in their own future – even what you might see as a small stake in risk assessment, because they're the ones facing the risks and to them it isn't necessarily that small – and they will respond accordingly.

Therefore, if you read back over this chapter, look for all the areas that suggest you involve others in your team. Treat them as equals, so that you engender a situation where everybody wins in health and safety, and nobody loses.

Raising the health and safety profile

Two colleagues were having a drink at the end of a day's managing.

'Do you think people really appreciate how important this latest health and safety drive is? I mean, do they take any notice? I'm quite disappointed by what I see happening – the staff just don't seem to have got the message at all.'

'Well, I've told my people. We covered it at the weekly meeting on Friday.'

'How did you do it – perhaps I might learn something?'

'No problem. I put it on the agenda … well, not exactly on the agenda, but under any other business … and told them about it. I mentioned it just after telling them about the note from the boss, and about the note about the whip-round for old Briggsy's leaving present.'

'How did they react? They must have had quite a few questions and comments, I would think.'

'Not really. Half of them had to get away before the end anyway and the rest were still talking about the possible job losses – but I recorded the fact I told them, in the minutes.'

'Yes … I see. I think I am learning something. By the way, how did you get on when you arrived this morning, now they've started resurfacing the car park?'

'I was furious! All I knew was in that silly memo they sent round weeks ago. I'd forgotten all about it and I had to park out on the street. I tore Derek off a strip – asked him if he thought I was a bloody mind-reader! He said I'd initialled it to show I'd read it, but you know, that's what you do to shift the paperwork.'

TELLING THE TRUTH

This chapter looks at how to raise the health and safety profile – in particular how to put together an effective promotional campaign for health and safety in an organisation. And not just any campaign, but a campaign whose messages get through and carry real weight.

The trouble is, the world is overloaded with messages. They are absolutely everywhere – on television, in newspapers, on the radio, on the Internet and in a whole variety of other places. Indeed, there are so many messages that it is difficult to know which ones to trust. To some extent people feel they have been overloaded with unreliable messages. It isn't always clear what's true anymore.

Probably because of this there's a wide scale cynicism about truth and communication. All too often the message that comes down from politics, the media – or even from management – turns out not to be true. In many organisations truth is a highly flexible – not to say malleable – commodity. So it's not surprising that it can be difficult to convince staff that you are serious about health and safety, or even to make space for health and safety messages amid the communication jungle.

Your job is to start convincing people that you really do take health and safety seriously because it is tremendously important, and that everyone has a part to play. If you don't get this message over then any attempt to establish a health and safety culture is doomed to failure. If you or your organisation has a record of false starts – say with customer care, quality or another 'flavour of the month' management issue – you have your work cut out to convince people that this time you are for real.

Oh, yes, and ... before you go any further, there's a question for you. Do you really believe in it yourself? Really? To the extent that you would defend the importance of health and safety if someone challenged you in the pub? If you don't, and you're trying to get other people to become involved in something to which you have no deep personal commitment ... forget it. Do not pass go, because they'll see through you in a second. Your credibility and the credibility of health and safety as a serious issue will be blown for good.

If you've read this far the chances are you have the commitment and the enthusiasm you need, so the first thing to look at is where you are now in terms of getting the message across.

WHAT ARE YOUR INFORMATION SYSTEMS LIKE AT THE MOMENT?

You need to get a feel for what kind of profile health and safety has at the moment and how it's promoted before you can start taking decisions about how to promote it better.

The following is a twelve point checklist that you should work through. It will give you an idea of how much needs to be done and help you start thinking through your tactics. As you go through it, answer whether the statement is entirely true, partly true, or definitely untrue for your organisation.

1 If I walked round my place of work I wouldn't find many notices or public mentions of health and safety.

2 Communication tends to be one-way – from the top downwards.

3 We don't really seem to be able to feed any messages upwards to our managers.

4 I can't remember the last time we had any health and safety training. Any that *we have had* was just to meet the needs of new legislation.

5 The way we communicate health and safety always seems to be done in the same kind of boring way.

6 We just have the usual poster inside the door and that's it.

7 No one is specifically responsible for publicising health and safety – it happens on an ad hoc basis.

8 There's no budget for publicising health and safety.

9 Health and safety notices are regularly daubed with graffiti or defaced.

10 Health and safety messages aren't translated into other languages.

11 When we need space on the notice board we tend to pin up any new messages over the health and safety posters or other notices.

12 We do have some health and safety communications around the place but they all tend to be about three or four years old. We haven't updated for a very long time.

What you answered of course will depend on your own organisation but it will give you an idea of where you are starting.

If you answered either entirely or partly true to most of it, it is clear that you are starting off from a very low base. Your organisation has a disorganised or even hostile approach to publicising health and safety and isn't showing much visible commitment to it. In this case you need to start thinking about putting something in place quickly to start turning things around.

If you answered mainly that these things were definitely untrue for where you work then you will be able to take slightly more time or build up a more refined strategy early on.

If you said they were all definitely untrue, either you're in an organisation that already has a positive health and safety culture, or you're wrong (the word 'lying' was considered, but it sounds a bit too blunt). Get to the point where you can say everything on that list is untrue and you're almost home and dry. So if you painted too rosy a picture, go back and have another look. There's no disgrace in being honest – because the truth is that most organisations fail miserably to measure up to questions like these.

THINKING THROUGH INFORMATION FLOWS

Before you can start planning how to raise the profile of health and safety at work in a detailed way, it's useful to get a picture of the way different aspects of information link together within organisations. Diagramatically it often looks like this.

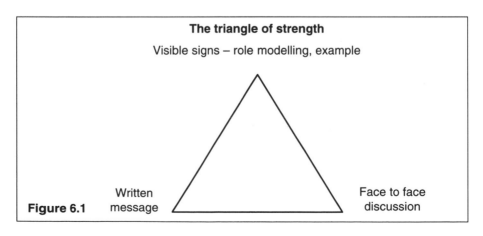

The triangle of strength

Visible signs – role modelling, example

Written message

Face to face discussion

Figure 6.1

This is useful because it shows that to get the health and safety message across you need to have a varied approach, which mixes a number of different things. It should include:

- the way you behave, your example and the visible signals you give about health and safety
- the written messages your organisation presents
- the face to face sessions that help get the message across forcefully.

It also shows that, to publicise your commitment to health and safety and raise its profile successfully, you need to have a consistent and constant approach – a triangle of strength. Take out one side and it falls to pieces, so all three sides are essential. It would be no good, for instance, saying all the right things in a written message or report if your behaviour or the tone of your conversations about the subject gave out conflicting messages. Each side of the triangle supports the other, and with this three point approach you can communicate a really powerful health and safety message.

6

Different directions

Another point worth considering is the need within a health and safety culture to get information flowing in different directions.

It doesn't always start out that way, though. This is the cast-iron way of raising the profile of health and safety because it attacks the issue from a number of different angles. Diagramatically it often looks like this.

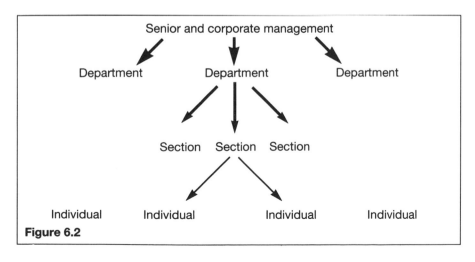

Figure 6.2

There's a one way, downward flow that cascades through the organisation. Unfortunately, the messages get weaker as they get lower, filtered out by people who select what they think other people need or have a right to know. It takes a long time – if ever – for information to get from the top of the cascade to the bottom.

The only effective way to get communication working is to aim for the flows shown on this diagram.

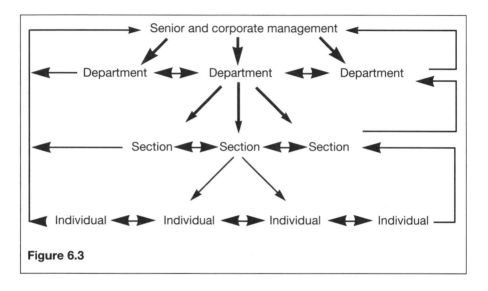

Figure 6.3

It looks a mess – because arrows are flying in every direction. There are even some missing, because each department should be talking to every other department, as should each section and individual. There are also links missing with the outside world, in and out at all levels.

What this diagram shows is that any successful publicity for health and safety happens:

● upwards

● downwards

● across.

In other words, the health and safety culture is built on the idea that information is constantly moving around an organisation. Messages come down from senior managers and they are backed up by action and example, so it's more than just orders and instructions to be obeyed on a 'do as I say, not as I do' basis.

This in turn encourages messages to come up from the front-line staff who are able and encouraged to feed back ideas about health and safety improvements and whether the actual policies are working. The third part of this virtuous triangle is that information is shared between teams, or in other words across the organisation. This means that teams themselves can look for ways of improving and getting the health and safety message across forcefully.

Now, at this point you may be feeling a little unsure – discouraged even, because the reality is that exceptionally few organisations operate like this at the moment. The chances are that yours doesn't either. There are commonly barriers between departments, functions and sections that make them feel like different empires, and any upward flows of ideas and information that do exist are limited to certain managers or are generally very weak.

This is actually encouraging. It's a no-lose situation. If your organisation is a model of effective communication, you can use this to very strong advantage. But even if it isn't, it means that there is only one way for things to go ... and that's up. Anything you do, including the ideas you can try which follow very soon, will make a positive improvement.

If you bear the two models and their diagrams in mind, you have the foundations to start building a coherent health and safety message – one that does the job effectively.

Different strokes for different folks

A final point that's worth stressing here when thinking about how to raise a profile, is that different parts of the organisation are likely to have different levels of responsibility for getting messages across, like this.

- Senior management is there to support and fund any communications strategy.

- Managers in the middle are generally there to interpret the messages that come down from senior managers. Their job is often to put health and safety initiatives and ideas into a language everyone understands. It's also their job to carry back up to senior managers messages that are coming through from front-line staff.

- Front-line staff are there to carry out health and safety messages and make sure everyone in the team is doing their bit and is fully aware of what's being said.

So wherever you are in an organisation you're likely to have responsibility for communicating health and safety messages and raising the profile of health and safety at work. If any of these tiers are missed out of the process, the chances are that the messages won't get through. If senior managers don't show commitment, then the chances are that any good ideas that come through won't actually get used in practice. If managers in the middle don't play a part they may well act as a block, crushing new ideas. If front-liners don't buy in the chances are that however good the message, however slick the campaign, however high the profile, in reality the sensible health and safety messages won't be carried out.

DEVELOPING A SIX POINT ACTION PLAN

The following is an approach to developing an action plan for raising the profile of health and safety at your organisation.

To raise the health and safety profile where you work your approach needs to be:

- **truthful**
- **adventurous**
- **regular**
- **geared towards your people**
- **energetic**
- **targeted.**

In other words you need to have a **target**. The following shows, how this model works in practice.

The truth, the whole truth and ...

People quickly notice if the messages you are trying to get across are inconsistent. This is why any message about health and safety must be absolutely truthful and backed up with action.

This principle of making sure your messages are truthful and match up with the reality of the company is very important when thinking through how to raise the health and safety profile where you work.

One way of looking at truthfulness is that any drive to raise the profile of health and safety needs to be led by example.

Managers need to demonstrate that they say what they mean and they do as they say. So, if your company is committed to giving people working on VDUs regular breaks, then it's important that you don't get blown off course the first time you have an overload situation at work.

Supporting the triangle of strength

The following are some of the things you can do to show that you're really serious about health and safety messages:

- chair meetings about health and safety yourself

- become actively involved in any accident or ill-health investigation

- do regular health and safety tours

- back up your actions with written messages where it's appropriate – not just memos, but posters, signs, leaflets

- discuss the issues one to one, as you go round on health and safety tours, or in everyday management.

6

Being adventurous

Variety, it is said, is the spice of life and this is certainly the case when it comes to getting messages across about health and safety. It's all too easy to put up a poster. Sure, posters do have their place, but it isn't enough just to go for the traditional and simple ways. Remember your health and safety messages are jostling for people's attention along with a whole range of other 'important' things.

What you really want is a broad and adventurous strategy towards getting the message across. This is how one company set about looking at an adventurous approach to communicating the health and safety message:

'We've done all kinds of things here. We had some mugs made with a health and safety message on them. We also ran a health and safety competition where there was a prize for the entry with the best ideas to improve things. We certainly didn't stop at the old way which was just to have the poster pinned up on one of the offices.'

Health and Safety representative

Making it fun

One of the real ways of getting through any health and safety message and raising the profile of health and safety is to make it fun. There's nothing worse than another dry and drab circular telling people what to do about health and safety. If it's fun and people feel involved they are much more likely to take notice.

This is how one health and safety inspector managed to make the message fun and therefore much more powerful.

'I always start off with a little talk about Albert and the lion – the old Stanley Holloway monologue where Albert decides to get into a lion's cage when he goes to the zoo and the lion eats him. In the end he gets out, but the point is that the first step to any health and safety is to know where the lions are and what they're capable of doing. In other words, you need to know what things are most likely to cause you harm. I use this as an easy way of getting into the whole business of risk assessment because it's fun and people can actually understand what I'm talking about.

When I've done this I then say there's another set of lions that you don't know about or can't see. For instance, what happens if you don't know how close together the bars are in this cage and you lean against it? You might put your arm through almost inadvertently. This translates in the following way: that you must know what you're dealing with and that means looking. If you don't know what the risks are, you can't tackle them seriously.'

This example is a good one because it shows how an adventurous approach to talking about a potentially dry subject like risk assessment can actually get the message through much more effectively.

Regular

People may well be committed to health and safety but it is easy to forget how important it is, particularly when work gets tough. When you begin to think about how to get the message across you need to update it constantly, and devise new ways of communicating it.

A lot of regular messages are much more effective than one big push that quickly peters out. A new emphasis on the message every week is one way of keeping health and safety right at the front of people's minds. This is how one organisation managed it.

Staying regular

The important thing for health and safety is to keep the messages coming regularly and to vary them. If you simply put up the same old poster or the same old message people are likely to lose interest or simply not see it any more because they're so used to it.

There are a variety of ways of keeping things regular but you may use things like team meetings, or sessions where you get together specifically to discuss health and safety issues or any near misses that you've had.

Geared

The most effective message is one that is designed with the audience in mind. It's very easy to become a subject-matter expert and focus just on the subject. For instance, in health and safety terms you may become an absolute expert in risk assessment but unless you can get the message over in an effective way to the people who need to hear it you remain in the realms of the out of touch expert. This is where the Albert and the lion example is so useful.

The important thing with any effort to raise the profile of health and safety is to tailor your message closely and clearly to the people who need to hear it. You need to ask yourself questions like:

- *what level of language should I use?*
- *how much detail should I go into?*
- *can I say it in an entertaining way?*

- *what will interest people?*
- *what will motivate people?*
- *what will gain people's commitment?*

Additional information or a deduction?

A medium sized engineering firm decided to put a leaflet on health and safety in everyone's salary envelope, with their statement of earnings.

Their view was that they had communicated – but communication happens when the message is received and the circuit completed, not just because a message has been sent.

Most people glanced at it and binned it – or used the back of it to work out whether their tax and NI was right. That was, after all, what they were interested in at the time.

The 3Ms

One useful way of looking at that list is in terms of the 3 Ms. The 3Ms stand for:

- **market**
- **message**
- **medium.**

This sounds a bit off-putting but the idea is very simple really. It works like this. Whenever you want to get a message across you need to think about three different things.

- The first M stands for market. Who are the people who will receive your message? What do they want? What are they looking for in your message? How should you pitch it to make sure you get it right for them?

- The second M stands for message and this is relatively straight-forward. What it means is you need to be clear about the message you want to communicate. What are the main things you want your audience to hear? What do you want to happen as a result?

- The third M stands for medium and again this is pretty straight-forward. A medium is a channel of communication, such as a report, memo, radio broadcast or speech. Selecting the appropriate medium means asking yourself, what's the best way of getting to people, what is the medium to which they will be most responsive?

Anyone for a pinta?

At one point the National Consumer Council wanted to get complaints procedures publicised more effectively. Many organisations were saying that consumers had to write in for a form on which to complain or else did not give out their phone number.

The then Chairman of the National Consumer Council, Lady Wilcox, made an interesting statement. She said that the best medium for complaints information was the tops of milk bottles. She said that service organisations should be able to print their phone number on milk bottle tops or on the back of bus tickets or train tickets, places which were really accessible so that people could immediately know where to phone up if they had a complaint or suggestion to make.

6

Sadly this particular suggestion wasn't taken up but it illustrates an important point. You need to make sure you get the right medium. So when you are thinking about doing your presentation you need to work through the 3Ms.

How not to

This is an extract from a health and safety leaflet given out to all visitors to a large organisation. Whoever wrote it hadn't done the 3Ms test first

1. DO NOT TAKE PERSONAL RISKS.
2. Do not take photographs unless authorised to do so.
3. CONTRACTORS must ensure that they are fully conversant with the 'Safety rules and regulations' to be observed by contractors working on our premises. If visiting the Data Centre, please refer to the special instructions for the Data Centre issued by Security at the reception desk.

For a start, for whom is this written – who is the market? It is written in bureaucratic language. The message is confused – the clause on photos is a health and safety red herring. And the medium – who is going to read through a detailed and dense leaflet if there is an emergency?

Energetic

Getting the message over takes energy and commitment. If you don't look as if you are enthusiastic about it then how do you expect your people to be enthusiastic? This doesn't mean taking a whole bunch of multi-vitamins and charging round like a maniac.

Instead you need to control it but make sure you've got reserves of energy when the going gets tough. You're bound to come across people who feel cynical about health and safety or who simply don't buy in. But if you can keep your enthusiasm and your energy up then its likely that you're going to win people over.

Targeted

This is the last of the six points. One of the reasons why messages about health and safety don't get home is that they are not delivered to the right people.

You need to be clear about who the opinion formers are in your organisation and then target these specifically with your health and safety message.

More about opinion formers

The reason you need to think about opinion formers is that attitudes on health and safety are often deeply ingrained. As part of the process of raising the profile of health and safety you may well need to change people's views about the way they ought to behave. They may have been behaving in an unsafe way at work for many years. Indeed, the organisation itself may have been encouraging them to behave this way or playing no active part in guarding their safety. This means that you'll need to start winning people over to your ideas and convincing them that the new ways are really better.

Obviously you can do this in part with written and other messages. But changing attitudes and raising the profile of health and safety is very much a hearts and minds exercise. This means you need to start spreading the message gradually to your team and your organisation. As with any change, some people will be enthusiastic, but many will feel threatened. This means that as part of the process of getting people to take health and safety more seriously, you need to start making them feel less frightened of change. And the best way to do this is to identify people who can carry your messages into the work force and show that it's OK to take health and safety seriously, like the following example from a building site.

'When I started at the building site no-one really took health and safety seriously. If you used barrier cream on your hands you came in for wide scale derision from your team mates. It wasn't thought to be very manly. Anyone using barrier cream was the butt of all jokes.

When I got promoted and the organisation really wanted to push home the health and safety message, one of the things we had to tackle was the whole business of deeply held macho attitudes. If I'd just gone along and done a poster or put up something saying people should use barrier creams, it would have been ignored like every other poster. The only way to do it was to identify people who could actively help get the message across.

The first thing I did was pick on a couple of the really tough guys who worked in the team and spend time working through with them why it was important. One really became enthusiastic and through him I started to raise the profile of health and safety. When everyone saw that he was taking it seriously and using barrier cream and gloves, they started taking it seriously too. We built on this to change the whole culture.'

6

You can look in a number of places for your opinion formers:

- **The out and out cynic**. Some people have such a negative block on any attempt to get the message over that you need to target them. In the first instance the aim is to get them to buy in to your communication process. You might want to talk to them individually or generally involve them in the process. If you can turn an agnostic into a believer it will help give you a powerful way of showing what you believe in. However, in the final analysis you may find that you simply cannot win these people over. In which case you will need to do all you can to marginalise them and make sure you can by-pass them effectively with messages.

- **The enthusiast**. You are likely to find people who are popular with their colleagues and are enthusiastic. These may well be people you can get to carry your message into your workforce effectively. You'll look at this area a little later when you look at how to manage the information grapevine.

Using health and safety representatives

Probably the greatest ally in any attempt to raise the profile of health and safety at work is a health and safety representative. All too often health and safety representatives are regarded as adversaries by managers in organisations. However, they should be seen as partners because they are people who are often trusted by front-line staff.

So, if you can work with your health and safety representatives to help get the message over into the work place all the better. Indeed, you should be asking your health and safety representatives how they think the message can be communicated more effectively and how you can raise the profile of health and safety. And of course, when you've listened, the important thing is to act. It's no good getting a whole range of useful suggestions if they either sit in your in-tray or stay in the back of your mind for the next six months.

One way of looking at your health and safety representative is as a kind of champion for the cause. This is the person who can spread the message most effectively because their commitment is assured. They are also most likely to be plugged into the grapevine. They will probably have a handle on when messages are being ignored and any good ideas that are coming through.

MAKING THE PLAN WORK

So you've looked at some important background areas in terms of getting your message across. But how do you make it work in practice?

The important thing is to have a publicity plan, and the way to start any plan is by asking yourself some questions, and giving yourself sensible answers. The following are six key questions you should address as you go about the business of deciding how to raise the profile of health and safety in the place where you work.

Why are we raising the profile of health and safety?
Whom do we target?
What are our specific objectives?
How do we intend to achieve them?
How will we know whether we've been successful?
When are we going to launch our campaign?

When you've answered these questions you can actually go about the business of putting some concrete plans in place.

It's important though not to get too hung up on producing a great master plan and attempting to change everything. You may well be able to implement many of your ideas quickly and simply and at very little cost. The important thing is to get the momentum going, and build up lots of many different messages and different ways of promoting health and safety at work.

SOME IDEAS FOR RAISING THE PROFILE

Always work on the personal benefits

Before you even start on a plan to raise the profile of health and safety at work there is one very important tip. You'll recognise the underlying message from the way you react to being told what to do, and from what you read about the need to strike a chord with individuals so they recognise what's in it for them.

6

All too often health and safety messages fail because they are far too dictatorial. People suddenly see a message or a poster or something on the wall that tells them what they *should* do. And people tend to react negatively to simply being *told* what to do. They often feel that a bald statement or message is an affront or an attack on the way that they've been doing things in the past and may well choose to ignore it.

It is much more effective to take a broad approach and treat people like grown-ups when you are trying to raise the profile. So you should not just be explaining what you require someone to do, you should also be explaining things in a way that strikes a chord with them.

> *Explain why it needs to be done.*

Organisations that treat health and safety effectively are those that help people to understand why it matters that they act in a healthy and safe way. They don't just tell people what to do, although there may be an element of setting down the rules.)

> *Be clear about when it needs to be done.*

People need to know when health and safety actions must to be carried out, they need to know whether there any exceptions or any room for manoeuvre.

> *Clarify what results are needed.*

People need to know what is expected of them.

At the heart of any health and safety culture is the belief that everyone has a role to play. If you simply present your messages as instructions, then the likelihood is people will consign them to the filing system they use for all messages in this vein ... the waste paper basket.

This simple psychological approach makes a lot of sense – as experience at the sharp end proves.

The following is how one health and safety inspector explained his successful approach:

'We used to go into this particular organisation and it had all the messages up. In one particular room people had to wear ear protectors. Every time I went there I walked in and staff would be working at their job with ear protectors neatly on the table. The boss would then follow me in and harangue them about putting their ear protectors on. They always said sorry and put the protectors on.

We'd leave the room and I'd sneak back 15 minutes later to find the ear protectors once more lying on the table. The only way I made any progress was to sit down and talk through with the people what was happening to them because they didn't wear ear protectors. When they understood that, they started to wear them.'

So far you have looked at a broad action plan and built up a picture of where you are at the moment in terms of your publicity. What you now need to do is develop a range of different ideas.

The following are just some practical tips and tricks for raising the profile of health and safety where you work.

Prune the grapevine

Whatever formal communication processes are in place, the informal network – the grapevine – is always going to be there. It's a function of any situation where a number of people work together. It cannot be removed but it can be monitored and controlled to a degree.

The information that flows around an organisation will be either accurate or rumour. By raising the level of the accurate information you reduce the room available for unfounded speculation, half-truth and invention. In other words, if you try and ensure that all appropriate information that is of interest to other people is fed into the system, the accurate will replace much of the rumour.

Mind you, the grapevine will always be working, so monitoring it and picking up the feel of what is being said is an excellent way of keeping a finger on the communication pulse.

Invent a slogan

Just think how powerful slogans can be in terms of getting your message across quickly and effectively. For instance, the slogan on the gates of every Butlins holiday camp is *Number One for Fun*. It's hard to think of a more effective slogan which gets across the message in just a few words.

Why not hold a competition to come up an effective health and safety slogan that will accurately and powerfully reflect the way and place that you work.

Publicise your philosophy

In many ways publicising health and safety philosophy is like a more serious version of a slogan. You can see a slogan as a throw-away thing. You could keep inventing new ones every week. However, a health and safety philosophy statement will be with you for a year or even longer. It's worth getting right, and worth realising how important such statements are.

The following are just some health and safety philosophy statements reported in *Successful Health and Safety Management* from the Health and Safety Executive.

A good safety record goes hand in hand with high productivity and quality standards.

We believe that an excellent company is by definition a safe company. Since we are committed to excellence it follows that minimising risk to people, plant and product, is inseparable from all other company objectives.

These are just two examples of powerful philosophy statements. Your organisation may already have such a statement or, if not, you need to start working on one. Remember the idea is that a statement will be something that can be put around the workplace and will mean something to people who read it.

Something to do

Write a health and safety philosophy statement for your team.

Suggestion schemes

Many organisations have suggestion schemes, where employees who see where improvements could be made, often fairly simply, feed their suggestions into the system. Suggestions come from the people who work most closely with the issues on which they are reporting, and this ensures that their specialist knowledge and personal insight are used to unlock a good deal of creativity.

The suggestions are evaluated and costed and, in most successful schemes, the employee is rewarded with a share or a percentage of any cost savings. In health and safety this may mean there is a direct and immediate saving or it may mean estimating the potential costs of a health and safety failure, and basing any reward on that nominal figure.

Where suggestion schemes score is by opening the door to an upward flow of information, on small issues that might otherwise never be mentioned. The fact that the scheme is always there makes it easy to make a suggestion while it's fresh in one's mind, rather than having to wait for a meeting or a special approach.

Run an ideas competition

Some organisations operate a variation on the suggestion scheme themes. They run competitions offering a prize for the best suggestion for improving health and safety at work. This of course gives you a number of opportunities.

On the one hand it allows people to feel a commitment to your message – it must be something the organisation takes seriously if they're doing this! On the other it gives you a fresh way of publicising health and safety when you come up with a new idea generated. So you get publicity at the beginning when you are launching the scheme, during it as you encourage people to take part and afterwards when you broadcast the ideas. It can also be a powerful motivator because success breeds success.

It supports the permanent suggestion scheme because it adds a special, one-off activity and therefore provides a sharp and time-limited focus.

Run a health and safety awards scheme

Award schemes are allied to suggestion schemes and ideas competitions. There are many examples in all sorts of areas – employee of the month, star department, and most improved section, for instance. You often see posters up with someone's photo, singling them out for special recognition. Jeremy Stranks in *Management Systems for Safety* explains that there are also examples of specific health and safety awards.

> *Whilst there are a number of national award schemes run by safety organisations such as the Royal Society for the Prevention of Accidents (RoSPA) and the British Safety Council, many organisations run their own internal award schemes.*

He illustrates the criteria for what he describes as a typical health and safety award scheme and puts forward a framework where:

- there are different levels of award – maybe gold, silver and bronze
- when the scheme starts there is room to add an extra level, to recognise the greatest improvement made
- the award should be prestigious, a shield or cup awarded annually, engraved with the names of each year's winners
- anyone winning the award also has permanent recognition – a plaque or certificate they can display
- like the Queen's Award to Industry, the winners in one year could

use a special logo or be allowed to fly a flag to show they have been winners.

The process for selecting people, units, departments or sections for consideration will naturally depend on local circumstances, but the way it is handled needs to demonstrate the seriousness with which the award is treated. Jeremy Stranks suggests that perhaps a senior manager should nominate those going forward for consideration, who are then assessed by a visiting judging team or panel.

Such a scheme has considerable potential for getting a very clear and strong message across. It certainly needs continuous publicity to get people keen to enter and to let them know what is happening at each stage. It might merit description – with photographs and details – in a company annual report, and in a special press release that goes to local and trade press. It could even form the basis of a special presentation evening – a sort of 'Safety Oscars' – really to raise the profile.

Publicising your health and safety policy

In many ways policies are the work horse of any health and safety drive. It is the policy that will determine where the organisation is going and what it expects of its people. If your organisation has five or more employees it must have a health and safety policy, by law, and it's good practice to have one, whatever the size of the firm. So dig it out and see whether you think it works.

The following is based on a checklist in *Successful Health and Safety Management* which looks at how to evaluate the effectiveness of health and safety policies.

Written statements of health and safety should at the very least:

- set a direction for the organisation by communicating senior management values, beliefs and commitments to health and safety
- explain the basis of the policy and how it can contribute to business performance (e.g. by reducing injuries and ill-health, protecting the environment and reducing unnecessary losses and liability)
- establish the importance of health and safety objectives in relation to other business objectives
- commit the organisation to pursuing progressive improvements in health and safety performance, with legal requirements defining the minimum level of achievement
- explain the responsibilities of managers and the contribution that employees can make to policy implementation, outlining the participation procedures
- commit the organisation to maintaining effective systems of communications on health and safety matters
- identify the director or key senior manager with overall responsibility for policy formulation, implementation and development
- commit the leaders of the organisation to supporting the policy with adequate financial and physical resources and by ensuring the competence of all employees and by the provision of any necessary expert advice
- commit the leaders to planning and regularly reviewing and developing the policy
- be signed and dated by the director or chief executive of the organisation.

6

Posters

In many ways the poster has been the bastion of health and safety publicity. Most organisations have a crumpled poster somewhere exalting people to wear hard hats, or take a break from the VDU screen or bear in mind different legislation. However, despite this, posters shouldn't be overly denigrated. A well designed poster can be a very powerful way of raising the health and safety profile. What you may want to do is open this up to the floor and run a poster competition. If one of your staff can design a poster it's much more likely to be effective than if one simply appears on the notice board from an official source.

The world's worst

Just think of some of the truly and monstrously unsuccessful communication initiatives. You will find that they share a lot of things in common, certainly things you will want to avoid as you go about getting the organisational message across. Take British Rail's *We're getting there* campaign. This was a disaster because it was ambiguous. People weren't quite sure what it meant and it certainly didn't conform with people's experience of travelling on British Rail. It failed the truthfulness test and so fell at the first hurdle.

Take Gerald Ratner's speech in which he described the goods he sold as 'crap'. This led to the demise not just of the company, but of Ratner himself who had to resign as Chief Executive. This was a terribly unsuccessful act of communication because Ratner did not think through clearly who his audience were. It may well have worked for the small audience of knowing city people he was addressing. However, when it got out to the general public, those people who actually bought the goods, it was perceived widely and quite rightly as a terrible insult. It failed the test of being geared towards an audience and indeed of being targeted properly.

And remember ... make the message fun

Eating the elephant

Marley Building Materials wanted to improve health and safety, and realised that at the very heart of this had to be a communications strategy. They decided to launch the Eat an Elephant Campaign. This was based on a simple slogan *You can't eat an elephant all at once*. They then launched a scheme whereby different parts of the organisation were given the task of eating one part of the elephant – in other words, with coming up with one idea that could improve health and safety.

At the end of every couple of weeks they held a public gathering at which the Chief Executive was able to hand out awards for the best elephant eating feat of that particular month. The idea was that this was fun, and lively, and it was inclusive. It also went well beyond the simple business of just putting up a poster and telling people they must improve health and safety.

Tying it in with something else

One of the reasons it can sometimes be difficult to get people to listen to your health and safety messages is that people think they are going to be dull and drab. Obviously you can tackle this by making it fun, which is something that we've looked at in detail in this section. Another way of getting over this barrier is to wrap up any attempt to raise the profile of health and safety with another initiative. This is how one organisation did it.

> 'We launched a big TQM initiative at work. We started to look at what it was our customers were looking for and ways we could improve our working practices. People got very excited by it and we put a lot of effort into making it work. As part of this TQM initiative, we also brought in health and safety.
>
> We did this by linking health and safety and quality, saying they're both about looking at ways to improve continuously how we work – to make it safer in one case and improve service to customers in the other. We were able to dovetail the two and as part of any agenda items or meetings we brought in health and safety messages and collected ideas from people. I don't think we would have been anywhere near as successful if we had just launched a health and safety drive.'

6

USING TRAINING

So far you have looked closely at raising the profile of health and safety through messages. Indeed, messages are important and they are a way of getting across what you believe in. But the bottom line is whether people change their behaviour.

There is no point raising the profile of health and safety if everyone is behaving in exactly the way they did before. This is where a programme of health and safety training can help – both raising the profile of health and safety and making it happen in practice.

A well-thought out programme demonstrates just by its existence that the organisation takes the issue seriously – nobody wastes money on non-essential training these days. It also helps clarify why health and safety matters to individuals and the organisation, and it gives people the hands-on skills they need to get it right.

So people begin to understand why health and safety is such an important issue, what role they have to play, and how they can play it.

RAISING THE PROFILE FACE TO FACE

You've looked at getting written messages across, starting up training, and leading by example to raise the profile of health and safety. The final part of this jig-saw is face to face meetings that can *really* help get the message over. If you don't use a face to face approach your written messages are likely to seem very sterile. They may well seem very official, and if you don't hold meetings and talk to people then they may not believe you are serious in them.

There is a variety of different ways to raise the profile of health and safety face to face. The following are just some ideas.

Team meetings and briefings

These are the standard work horse of any attempt to raise the profile of health and safety. In them you can get people together, talk about health and safety issues, collect ideas that move the process on.

Putting down health and safety issues on the agenda at all management meetings

One way of doing this is to make health and safety the first item on any management agenda and therefore show how important it is by making time to talk about it. All too often it's relegated to the end or any other business when you're already bored with the meeting or need to rush off to do something else. Where something comes on an agenda gives a strong message about its priority.

Monthly toolbox meetings

The idea of these is that you can get together with your health and safety representatives, supervisors, and other front-line staff, and talk through some positive ideas. In many ways this is how Marley Building Materials approached health and safety with its Eat an Elephant initiative. It's here that you can also talk about risks and other approaches.

Set up a health and safety action group

The idea is to create an active interest in health and safety. It should also reduce occupational ill-health and accidents. You can do this by:

- discussing and coming up with specific policy recommendations on health and safety issues for management

- working to get the recommendations approved by management and put into practice

- discovering unsafe conditions and practices and coming up with steps to tackle them

- teaching basic aspects of health and safety practice to group members who will then teach them to all staff.

Ideas sheet for raising the profile

Try to develop a sheet where you write down as many different ideas as possible for getting the message across. It's important to be broad and not just to drive everything from the top. Of course you will want messages to get through, but the key is for people to develop an ownership of these messages themselves.

6

THE TRAINING EVENTS

You looked earlier at the importance of backing up any messages with actual training. Hands-on training helps people apply some of the theories and ideas of a health and safety culture to the actual experience of their own work and situation.

But how do you get people to take health and safety training seriously? All too often training is seen as something someone else should do and something that can be skipped if people get busy elsewhere.

A number of different areas should be taken into consideration here. One of the problems with health and safety training is that it is perceived in many organisations to be an added extra, the kind of thing that can often be dropped as soon as people become busy.

If you can integrate the health and safety aspects of training into the core experience of the company, it will start to take it seriously. One of the ways to get people to turn up to training events and therefore spread the message about health and safety may be to call it something other than health and safety training.

For instance, you may well be able to include a health and safety element in all kinds of different training. Whenever you introduce a new piece of equipment or are developing an initiative such as quality, you could well be able to tie in a health and safety angle to this training.

There are other points you need to attend to as well – the same sort of motivation issue you looked at when you were exploring the issue of not ordering people about, if you want them to take it seriously.

'If it's good enough for me ...'
Fair point. If they have to go, where are the people above them?

Be there yourself – at least for enough of the time to demonstrate that you care about the issue. Otherwise it can turn into a 'do as I say, not as I do' situation in the eyes of your workforce.

'Why am I expected to attend?'
It's no good simply putting up a notice about health and safety training without making it absolutely clear whom the training is designed to benefit and what the benefits are. Only when you have done this are people clear who is expected to attend. They will then commit themselves to going, and you can hold them to attending.

In other words, you need to answer their unspoken questions – what's the point, what will I learn or be able to do in future that I can't do now? What's the deal? Why me?

In short, the best way to gain the commitment of others and develop their involvement, is to lead the way by example. If you don't play your part, nothing much else will happen.

And always step into the audience's shoes. Think what will motivate them to attend and tell their workmates to attend. And make it interesting when they get there.

The following is a real life example.

> *'I suppose we knew we had a health and safety problem at work. The problem was we were so busy that it just took a low priority. One day my boss came in and said:*
>
> *"Right, I've booked you on to a health and safety course next week."*
>
> *I was given no details about what the course was or why I was being told to attend. What's more I was stressed out with having so much work.*
>
> *On the day I came up with an excuse not to go.'*

6

Making it work for you

Two colleagues were having a drink after a hard day's managing.

'That health and safety consultant's report is amazing! There's so much to do. How do you think we can go about it?'

'I don't think there's any point. There's just so much that has to be started all at once that I think we'd go round and round in circles. I'm going to suggest we leave it. We've got away without a serious accident so far.'

'Yes, but we can't really do that. It wouldn't be right.'

'Don't go on about it. It's been a long day and my brain can't cope. Here comes the food – mine's the jumbo steak please.'

'Good grief! What a plateful! You'll never get through all that.'

'You just watch. If I take my time I'll do this justice. I can always get you to help me out if I need to. And anyway, as one of my ex-bosses used to say, the only way to eat an elephant is one spoonful at a time.'

In this last chapter we'll work through some ideas that can help you develop the health and safety behaviour and culture you are looking for at work.

This is important, of course, because the whole focus of any successful health and safety culture is:

● changing things

● moving you on

● getting things done.

It isn't an academic or 'feel-good' exercise. It is about changing perceptions and practices. The outcomes are obvious, but the motivation must be to make things work for you.

The issues you have looked at so far are the ones you need to work on in a health and safety culture. In 1991 the Confederation of British Industry (CBI) published *Developing A Safety Culture*. It identified from examples of good practice the features and characteristics that were prevalent in organisations where the health and safety culture was positive. It says that an organisation wishing to improve its performance needs to judge its existing practices against the following 11 point checklist of features. Look at it and you'll see we have stressed them all, as key components.

1 Leadership and commitment from the top which is genuine and visible. This is the most important feature.

2 Acceptance that it is a long-term strategy requiring sustained effort and interest.

3 A policy statement of high expectations and conveying a sense of optimism about what is possible, supported by adequate codes of practice and safety standards

4 Health and safety should be treated as other corporate aims, and properly resourced.

5 It must be a line management responsibility.

6 Ownership of health and safety must permeate all levels of the workforce. This requires employee involvement, training and communication.

7 Realistic and achievable targets should be set and performance measured against them.

8 Incidents should be thoroughly investigated.

9 Deficiencies revealed by an investigation or audit should be remedied promptly.

10 Consistency of behaviour against agreed standards should be achieved by auditing and good safety behaviour should be a condition of employment.

11 Management must receive adequate and up to date information to be able to assess performance.

TECHNIQUES FOR MAKING PROGRESS

Before constructing a detailed health and safety action plan focusing on your own situation and your own objectives, we need to look at some techniques which you can use to make the implementation more manageable and less difficult. There will be times when you feel it is virtually unmanageable, because change is like that, and there will be occasions when you wonder why you ever started. However, with careful thought and the use of some practical approaches, you can control the processes successfully.

Remember though that changing the way people behave and think is never easy. Think about how difficult you yourself find it to change.

Changing and developing culture has nothing to do with quick fixes. It is a long-term commitment to continuous improvement. This can make it seem a massive and amazingly complex set of issues, with no loose end to pick out so you can start to unravel it. Simply, where does one start? The following give you some ideas for the kick-off.

The important thing though is to start, however small (you look at this in more detail later). Remember that the only way to eat an elephant is to eat one leg at a time!

7

Build a health and safety team

Tackling anything major without support is lonely, frustrating – and generally leads to failure. Apart from anything else, developing a culture is about enhancing behaviour, so it pays to have as many like-minded souls on board with you as possible when you start the journey of continuous improvement.

It is clear that everyone eventually has to share ownership of health and safety, or it won't develop and stick. But you can't leave it to everyone to work individually on what they think needs doing. There has to be some co-ordination or the process will turn into anarchy or disillusionment.

Think about setting up a steering group, or a project implementation team, drawn from people whom you know are committed. The team could include managers, but it should also have some employee representatives, maybe union representatives if they exist in the organisation. The best teams often come from all levels and corners of the organisation, and include front-line workers, supervisors, canteen staff and people from every process.

Remember, though, this is not just another committee. This is a team put together to drive a specific project, and that makes it different from any ordinary group. A team has to work together to achieve a common purpose. This sounds simple, but it is essential to build a team on these main principles – working together, common purpose.

Behind these principles are some vital characteristics that differentiate project teams from other groups, including:

- a clear sense of direction and a set of agreed objectives

- appropriate leadership

- the ability to express different opinions in a climate of mutual support, trust, and openness, without rancour or scoring points

- the right mix of people – not all with the same skills and personal style, but a blend that gives you complete coverage

- a regular focus on how the work is going and how the team is doing.

You have seen the cycle in the next diagram before. Now, though, an extra dimension has been added. It isn't an extra stage – it's a function of the team as it works on the stages in the cycle, regularly and frequently reviewing progress and performance. The aim is to keep control of what is happening and tighten up quickly if anything needs adjustment. Taking early action nips in the bud problems and issues that would otherwise grow and turn into major difficulties.

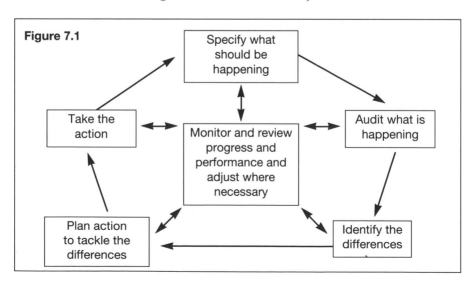

Figure 7.1

Specify what should be happening

Take the action

Monitor and review progress and performance and adjust where necessary

Audit what is happening

Plan action to tackle the differences

Identify the differences

If you want to look more closely at your role in leading such a health and safety team, refer to *How to Lead a Winning Team* by Morris S., Willcocks G. and Knasel E. (Pitman, 1995).

Let's put our cards on the table; teams are magic. They add up to far more than the sum of their parts. Run effectively, teams help you to:

- generate turbo-charged ideas
- work on solutions
- get things changed.

Teams can help influence popular opinion, sparking off the fundamental changes in attitudes which you are trying to achieve.

Pilot projects

Selecting an area, department, unit or section as a pilot project for the team to work on is an extremely effective way of:

- securing positive outcomes that can be reported back to influence the thinking of top managers
- learning about what does and does not work as you try to develop health and safety
- keeping the workload to manageable proportions
- increasing the chances of initial success
- starting the easiest option, and using success there to breed success elsewhere.

Using one part of the organisation as a test bed keeps the process simpler and allows you to make mistakes without blowing it completely. It also has a very strong effect on the communication profile – especially the grapevine aspect – as the people taking part in the pilot tell colleagues about it. If their experience is a positive one, then reassuring messages spread through other departments and functions, and make any extension of the pilot that much easier. Good experiences generate further demand, as those not involved at this stage begin to want the chance to develop the same sort of improvements for themselves.

But beware, if you are going to run a pilot, make sure you are serious about it and actually make changes in the light of the findings. If you test things out, you need to demonstrate that the test was worth it.

This is how one person described the pitfalls of piloting projects where she worked:

'I worked in the NHS for 25 years. People used to say that the NHS was the only place where pilots never land!'

Think about it ...

You have a team, you have identified a suitable pilot area, and you are sitting down with your team to draw up a strategy for progress. Where would you start?

The logical starting point would be the gaps between what is and what should be, as identified in some sort of audit.

However, if the task still looks gargantuan, one approach is to take the big picture to pieces.

Break down the problem

In order to effect change, the whole picture may have to be broken down into manageable components, so that realistic and achievable objectives can be set and met along the way.

One approach is to use a mapping exercise. This starts with putting the whole problem in the centre of a large sheet of paper. Off the central problem draw lines to smaller component problems. From these smaller problems, draw more lines to their smaller component issues. The following diagram is just one small part of such a map.

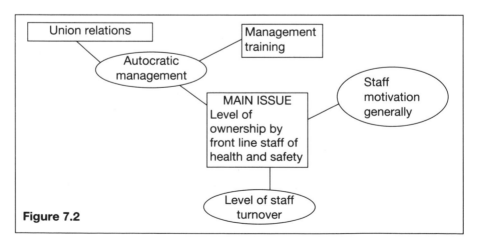

Figure 7.2

Identifying the issues in a map like this is best done in your health and safety team, to encourage the flow of ideas, and ensure that you can draw on as wide a range of expertise as possible.

Another technique often applied in change management is known as Force Field Analysis.

Force Field Analysis

This technique was devised by a management thinker and writer in the 1950s, Kurt Lewin. His starting point was that change is difficult because two opposing and equal sets of forces hold the status quo where it is. One set of forces drives change, the other set resists any change. Even if one set is stronger than the other and some change takes place, they will eventually equal each other out and the situation will be frozen where it is, the proverbial irresistible force and the immovable object.

Lewin proposed five stages in a process for destabilising the status quo, and working out where to put your energies to achieve the greatest impact for the least effort. The stages are these.

7

Define the problem

Work out what is wrong now and make sure you have as clear and quantifiable a picture as you can achieve. Imagine, for instance, that the problem is that people insist on taking a shortcut through a loading area, where forklift trucks are working, to the canteen. This is despite notices saying it is not a right of way and an instruction to the loading bay supervisor to stop people. You need to identify when it happens, how often, who is involved, what the results could be and anything else that proves it really is a problem.

If you're working on it with other people, make absolutely sure you all have precisely the same view of what needs to be changed.

Design the ideal scenario

Specify exactly what the situation would look like if you were to remove the problem. Get a picture in your mind of how it would be, and make the desired outcome as specific and measurable as you can.

Again, if you're looking at the issues in a group, ensure you're all aiming for exactly the same outcome.

Identify the forces

Now, list all the forces that are helpful in making the change (what Lewin called 'driving forces') and all those that are holding it back ('restraining forces'). Don't try and analyse them – just list them.

You may identify, for instance, that amongst the driving forces are:

● top management instructions that people must not walk through the loading area

● requests from the forklift drivers that someone does something to keep unauthorised people out of their work area

● a union representative who is safety conscious and keen to see the situation changed

● a near miss incident that you can use as a hook on which to hang the issue.

On the other side, the restraining forces could include:

● the fact that the route through the loading area has become accepted as normal over a three year period because there has been no attempt to raise health and safety awareness through training

● the lack of any other route, without going outside and round the building in the rain and cold

● the fact that the managing director is seen using the route frequently

● an ineffectual loading bay supervisor who is very reluctant to tell people to stop and go back – anything to avoid confrontation.

There will be others, naturally, but these are the sort of issues that push for and against change.

A chart (Figure 7.3) is normally used to list the drivers and restrainers. The status quo is the centre line, the desired position is the line to the right, and the drivers and restrainers face each other across the centre. By lengthening or strengthening the arrows (we've strengthened those in the example) you can indicate which forces are stronger than others. This helps at the next stage.

Prioritise the forces

Next, identify the main forces working for and against you, by analysing which ones would make the biggest impact if they were

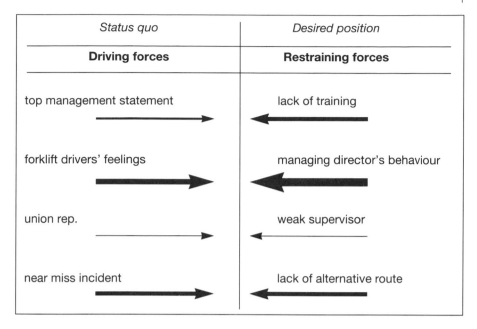

Status quo	Desired position
Driving forces	**Restraining forces**
top management statement	lack of training
forklift drivers' feelings	managing director's behaviour
union rep.	weak supervisor
near miss incident	lack of alternative route

Figure 7.3

7

removed or strengthened (depending on whether they're restrainers or drivers). Add weight to the ones which matter most and then identify which are easiest to remove or strengthen. Work out which have the most impact and counterbalance each other, and shortlist three or four.

In the diagram above only a few are shown and their priority has been depicted by using thicker lines. You can see that four drivers and four restrainers are seen to be important.

Plan a strategy

The strategy is about weakening the restrainers and strengthening the drivers, so that the status quo is destabilised and the situation unfreezes. For each force in your shortlist, work out a way of affecting it in the direction you need – as simply and positively as possible. In the example, there is no need to do anything about top management's stated view – it has already been made clear and can be used without any extra effort. However, all the others need some degree of attention, maybe in the following ways:

- use the near miss as a major issue for forcing the change – issue a new instruction that the incident has brought the problem to light and in the interests of everyone's safety and the forklift drivers' working efficiency, walking through the area will be considered grounds for disciplinary action in future; this can be linked to the top management statement to beef it up

- use the union official to support the supervisor, making them aware that unpopularity with the people who walk through the area is less of a problem than unpopularity with their own people, the union representatives and other more senior managers.

Providing an alternative route may be a factor with a huge potential impact on the problem, but it is likely to be the one that is most difficult to achieve. Still, the biggest restrainer is probably the managing director doing exactly what others are being told they must not, and she has to be confronted with this and reminded of her impact as a role model on other people's behaviour – politely and constructively, of course. Maybe if the MD has to walk round in the wet and cold a covered walkway might not be impossible to achieve?

Even without an alternative route, the strategy for the other forces is likely to get you to where you want to be, so it should not matter too much anyway – except that you need to be aware that there will be some discontent over it, especially during the winter. The MD needs to be warned in advance as well, as this is an issue that needs consideration as soon as it has been recognised. After all, the employees do have a point.

Finally, check that the strategy you devise can achieve what you wanted it to achieve when you started – things have a habit of drifting off course if you aren't careful, so a final check is always worthwhile. Then go to it.

The sum of the parts

What the Force Field Analysis has done is give you greater control of a complex problem, by breaking it down into factors. Each factor is manageable and important, while together they have caused an insoluble problem for months. It's no surprise that the greatest factor in the example was the behaviour of the managing director, and that virtually all the other factors were about how people behaved, rather than machines, equipment or money.

The other key factor centres on training. No training has taken place to develop an understanding of the risks involved, or the potential costs to individuals if an accident were to occur. Additionally, maybe some management training for the supervisor would strengthen their resolve.

Health and safety training is a critical factor in positive health and safety.

TRAINING FOR A SAFER WORKPLACE

Unless people are trained in health and safety, you have no right to expect them to know what is required, how to operate safely and what action to take when they are at work and find a potential problem.

There are several areas where training is essential no matter what else is happening – control of substances hazardous to health (COSSH) and fire precautions and procedures, for instance.

Training not only helps individuals develop their skills and knowledge, it sends a message to the organisation. If health and safety training is a high priority, is treated seriously, and takes place in pleasant surroundings, with obvious care, this says to everyone that here is an issue we take seriously. If it's tacked on to the end of a Friday afternoon, delivered by people who clearly have no interest (and sometimes little expertise), and seen as a necessary evil, then the status of the issues is zero before you start.

Similarly, the content and style of health and safety training affects the way it is perceived. If it is always factually-based and a process where one person talks at everyone else, it becomes boring, a chore and an absolute waste of time. The best that can be said of it is that someone can tick it off in a book as having been done – with no attention to how well or with what effects.

So, training is a cultural issue as well. The way it is handled reflects either a directive or a participative management style – and what you're aiming for is involvement, participation and commitment from everyone.

Using training creatively

If you are going to get people together, it makes sense to gain maximum benefits from the inevitable time and cost. This means involving people so that they are challenged and interested, because failing to do this will simply undo any of the progress made in raising the health and safety issue as a priority.

People often forget that training must be interesting. They stand up and lecture or mumble or drift off the point or talk too much. It is not uncommon for training to send trainees to sleep or, worse still, to bunk off before the day is over (maybe after the afternoon coffee break). One health and safety trainee memorably described the following scene drawn from a training session on health and safety he had attended.

'It was amazing. We started off with a lecture. Then the trainer showed a series of detailed slides that he read out to us. I kept thinking why just read things out, we could have done this at home Eventually we dragged along to lunch. By this time there was a hint of desperation about the proceedings. We were simply bored and uncomfortable with sitting still for so long. A bit of group work would have at least allowed us to stretch our legs and feel involved in what was happening. In the afternoon I counted three people actually asleep with one person snoring loudly.

The problem was that people left vowing never to do any more health and safety training and confirmed in the wrong impression that health and safety is dead boring.'

Do not follow this devil's guide. It shows exactly what you shouldn't do – at least if you want your health and safety training to be a success.

The devil's guide to health and safety training

- Organise the training at short notice so it is very difficult for people to attend.

- You do all the talking.

- Read out from your slides.

- Don't bother with group work.

- Don't ask for any questions.

- Run over into the breaks – which you can then cut back to a minimum.

- Keep it strictly factual.

- Don't have fun at any cost.

- Discourage variety.

- Discourage participation

- Stick to what you planned to do whatever happens.

Doing it yourself

Quite often, health and safety training has to focus on procedures and systems that ensure safe working. However, the key is to help trainees own the issues, so they successfully translate theoretical learning into practical action. Running training sessions yourself not only can be cost-effective, it also sends a clear message about your commitment and that of the organisation, and encourages this practical translation.

In a training session that aims to increase ownership, the trick is to enable people to make their own inputs and come up with their own answers, so that they are part of the process of designing procedures and systems and are committed *to* making them work. For anyone, *my* solution is better than *their* solution – even if the solution is apparently exactly the same. Not only does this participative approach engender greater ownership and commitment, it also harnesses the expertise of the people closest to the problem.

The chances are that front line workers are pretty clear about the problems, and the systems and procedures needed to sort them out. Almost certainly, they have worked out how to put things right … but nobody has ever asked them. As they know the issues from the inside, try and use their expertise and knowledge. You may need to tweak the end result so it conforms with best practice, but you can guarantee that the participative approach will elicit ideas and structures that get you either right to the target, or at worst very close.

What you do will depend on your own situation, but here are a couple of approaches that have been proved to work. You can see that each is participative and very simple. However, the results of group discussion and feedback could astound you, in terms of the common sense that emerges and the commitment it engenders.

A question of quality

Put people into small groups and ask them to spend a few minutes discussing what health and safety has to do with quality.

Let them have a couple of minutes to present their ideas to the other groups and open up a discussion, summarising at the end.

The sort of issues you want to come out (and can draw out if they don't appear without a little prompting) include:

- not having an accident is like quality, in that it means getting it right first time, every time

- failures in health and safety cost money, as do failures in quality, from reworking, scrap, downtime, investigations and all the issues you looked at under costs and benefits

- quality and health and safety both cut across departmental, occupational and hierarchical boundaries – what one person does has a potential impact on someone else; in the case of quality, someone sending incorrect part-finished products into the next department means that department can't do its job; in the case of health and safety, one person leaving a hazard in place means someone else will probably end up getting hurt – and accidents don't differentiate between front-line workers, directors, or people in different functions

- quality management is about searching for continuous improvement, in the same way as real health and safety

- both are situations where either everybody wins or everybody loses

- both are issues that involve everyone in looking after their own performance and practice, and helping other people to look after theirs, as an area of common and mutual interest

- people get a buzz from getting it right and from playing a creative part in identifying where they can influence their own work and its environment – and this leads on to the second approach.

Where are we now?

In small groups, get people to:

1 identify the accidents and incidents that occur most frequently in their work areas, or have happened more than once

2 think about the common factors in each case

3 work out what needs to happen in order to reduce the odds of it happening again

4 put together a simple procedure to make the situation safer.

There are several powerful strands in this apparently simple approach. For example, it:

- is a basic form of hazard spotting and the start of a risk assessment
- is linked to a cycle of continuous improvement – learning from experience and avoiding repetition of problems (another quality issue)
- involves everyone in a creative and practical activity that allows them to express what they already knew and were only holding back because nobody ever asked them. Involvement is a very powerful weapon in any successful training event.

Remember, don't be put off from running your own training events. No longer is training seen as the exclusive preserve of the professional trainer or training company – although, of course, external trainers can do a very good job for you. The important thing is to have confidence, be organised and enjoy it.

Buying it in

Large numbers of health and safety training packages are available. There are specialist trainers who can come in to work with you, courses and seminars at outside venues, and open learning, interactive video and computer packages on the market. It is always worth talking to your local Training and Enterprise Council about what is on offer, and about ways in which they may be able to help subsidise or fund a health and safety training package.

It's also worth finding out what training and learning materials HSE has produced or sponsored, given its key role in the UK health and safety scene.

Outside training providers bring an extra element to the process, in that they have expert knowledge where the training is about specific procedures, systems and requirements. But if the drive is for cultural change, always think first how you can do it yourself, or work with an outside consultant in arranging and delivering a programme – remember the impact of your own involvement.

Practical details

When one health and safety training event goes wrong it pollutes everything else in the same area. All health and safety training is tarred with the same brush and potentially written off. The commonest failures, though, occur in some of the simplest issues – 'domestic' arrangements, rather than the way the course was delivered.

One frequently cited problem is the low quality of pre-course or pre-training workshop briefing. Participants don't know what to expect and the fear of the unknown – or an assumption that it will be a boring lecture – means they spend days trying to get out of it and conjuring up their worst fears about it. Any potential benefit has been destroyed well before the event happens.

Anyone going for health and safety training first needs simple and accurate information, such as:

● advance warning, so they can programme it in

● clear and simple information on where it is, how long it lasts, what the breaks and the finishing times are, whether they need to take anything

● what the topic is, and what they will be able to do or will know after the training that they can't do now.

These are effectively 'hygiene factors'. They don't add to the motivation of trainees if they're right, but they clearly wreck involvement if they are not covered properly. It's the trivial details that seem to matter most, in some situations.

> **Think about it ...**
>
> *When you have been on a course and coffee is promised for 11.00 a.m., how do you feel when 11.10 comes round and you're still in the seminar room? How much of your attention is on the topic and how much on counting down the minutes to the break? What effect does this tiny detail have on the learning that you achieve and your feeling about the overall course?*

It matters! Issues like this have a disproportionate effect on people's attitude. As it's their attitude you are trying to change through health and safety training, you do have to get the details right. Similarly:

- never arrange health and safety training for a group of people and cancel it at the last minute
- never pull someone off a course just before it starts, because you can't spare them
- never go along and drag someone out of a session to answer a question or take a phone call.

If you do any of these or similar things, you contradict your own message. Arranging the training becomes meaningless, as your behaviour on the day clashes with your earlier insistence on attending the event. Your actions deny its importance.

Checking success

It is important to get feedback on any training sessions that your people attend or that you run yourself. This feedback is often in the form of 'happy sheets' where individuals note down their perceptions of a particular training event. If you've identified a weak event run by external people, don't keep sending other people to it. It's not just a waste of money, it turns people right off health and safety.

On the other hand, if it's an event you run yourself and there are some comments that imply it could be better or more effective, look at it in terms of continuous improvement. Take the comments, think about them, and improve next time, using the information you have been given.

If training is to meet its purpose, the feedback has to go further than whether the room was warm, the handouts readable and the tutor a good laugh. If the event was to increase the competence of those handling dangerous materials, then the long term effects should be monitored and evaluated.

THE HEALTH AND SAFETY ACTION PLAN

Putting together an action plan to develop a positive health and safety culture is a process that you should find relatively straightforward. It consists essentially of an auditing approach, with the added dimension that you should indicate what action will help you bridge the gaps.

It may be something you need to discuss in a team, as allocating specific tasks to people has to be done through negotiation and agreement.

The auditing approach

The CBI checklist gives us a ready-made standard against which to judge current performance and identify the gaps, although of course you are free to draw up your own.

As you see the checklist unfold, analyse each of the questions and make notes to represent your answers. Leave any questions you aren't sure about, and complete them once you have had the chance to research the situation. Remember, there are no right or wrong answers. The purpose of the exercise is to provide you with a tool you can use to plan and take appropriate action to develop a positive health and safety culture. Some criteria will need more attention than others – for instance, we haven't left a lot of space alongside the acceptance of cultural change as a long-term process. There isn't really that much to say.

ACTION PLAN	
Leadership and commitment from the top which is genuine and visible.	
The specific activities, issues, and tasks which are gaps that need tackling:	The specific action I/we intend to take to fill these gaps is:

7

Acceptance that it is a long-term strategy requiring sustained effort and interest.	
The specific activities, issues, and tasks which are gaps that need tackling:	The specific action I/we intend to take to fill these gaps is:

A policy statement of high expectations and conveying a sense of optimism about what is possible, supported by adequate codes of practice and safety standards.	
The specific activities, issues, and tasks which are gaps that need tackling:	The specific action I/we intend to take to fill these gaps is:

Health and safety should be treated as other corporate aims, and properly resourced.	
The specific activities, issues and tasks which are gaps that need tackling:	The specific action I/we intend to take to fill these gaps is:

It must be a line management responsibility.	
The specific activities, issues and tasks which are gaps that need tackling:	The specific action I/we intend to take to fill these gaps is:

7

Ownership of health and safety must permeate all levels of the workforce. This requires employee involvement, training and communication.	
The specific activities, issues and tasks which are gaps that need tackling:	The specific action I/we intend to take to fill these gaps is:

Realistic and achievable targets should be set and performance measured against them.

The specific activities, issues and tasks which are gaps that need tackling:	The specific action I/we intend to take to fill these gaps is:

7

Incidents should be thoroughly investigated.

The specific activities, issues and tasks which are gaps that need tackling:	The specific action I/we intend to take to fill these gaps is:

Deficiencies revealed by an investigation or audit should be remedied promptly.	
The specific activities, issues, and tasks which are gaps that need tackling:	The specific action I/we intend to take to fill these gaps is:

Consistency of behaviour against agreed standards should be achieved by auditing and good safety behaviour should be a condition of employment.	
The specific activities, issues, and tasks which are gaps that need tackling:	The specific action I/we intend to take to fill these gaps is:

Management must receive adequate and up to date information to be able to assess performance.	
The specific activities, issues, and tasks which are gaps that need tackling:	The specific action I/we intend to take to fill these gaps is:

7

Index

accidents   32
  costs of   39–41, 42–43
action plan
  making an   54–55, 86–87, 109–112, 182–190
  making it work   150–151
  profile, raising the   151–159
  six-point   142–150
analysing accidents   36–38
asbestos   31
attitude problems   53
audit
  carrying out an   58–60, 82–86
  continuous improvement   for, 96
  organisational safety   62–73
awards schemes   155–156

behaviour
  changing   68, 90–91
  checking   68–69, 84–85
  health & safety   72–73

choice, free   2
competitions   154–155
continuous improvement   60–62
costs
  accidents, of   39–41, 42–43
  non-financial   44–45
  positive health & safety, of   45–47
credibility factor   96–97
culture
  change   9–10, 68
  identifying an appropriate   79–81
  people and   90–91
  positive culture, benefits of   20–21

visible and invisible	64–73
days lost	
injury, number of	17
national picture	38–39
delegation	1–3
do nothing approach	2–4
do what you say you'll do	67
economic balance	47
employee, effects on the individual	43–44
environmental issues	31
expense or investment	14–16
experts, leaving it to	3–4
falls at work, numbers of people injured by	17
forecasting	22
force field analysis	171–175
health	30–32
health & safety	
behaviour	72–73
benefits of	12–13
identifying the	6–7
continuous improvement	60–62
do nothing approach	2
integrating, into the business	92
manager's attitude to	1–2
policy, building the specification	73–82
positive approach to, cost and benefits of	6–14
positive culture	
benefits of	20–21
purpose of	5
quality links with	20–21
selling	12
hygiene factors	131–132
implement your policy	67
improvement, continuous	60–62
incidents	32–33

analysing 36–37
individual, effects on 43–44
induction, conscious 106–107
information
    flow of 138–140
    systems, shape of 137–142
insurance 16–17
investing in health & safety 95–96
investment or expense 14–16

law, reasons for 53
leadership 99–100
lifting injuries, numbers of people sustaining 17

management
    better 132–133
    holistic approach to 5
    middle 8–9, 101–105
    senior 91–101
    supervisors and front-line 105–108
    top 8
measuring, conducting an audit 58–60
minimal approach, problem with 53
monitoring 95
motivators 131–132

obstacles, overcoming 102
organisational responses 10–11
organisational safety audit 62–73
    best practice, clarity about 62–63

personal responsibility 1–2
persuading the bosses 23–24
PESTEL technique 21–22
pilot projects 169
plan See action plan
policy
    building the specification 73–82
    culture, identifying an appropriate 79–81
    drawing the specification together 81–82

external sources 74–76
internal sources 76–79
practice and 25–26
posters 157–159
pressure, adding 69–70
prevention 34–36
passive, is not 6
problem solving 171
procedures, co-ordinating 97–98
profile, raising the 151–159, 160–161
progress, making 167
publicising the policy 158

quality approach, benefits of 18
quality management 5
health & safety, links with 20–21
modern approach 19–20
old-fashioned 18–19
positive culture, benefits of 20–21

responsibility
clarifying 94–95
personal 1–2
shared 3–5
reviewing 95
risk assessment 114–129
bridge to a health and safety culture, as 129–134
calculating 123–125
culture and 133–134
risk, reducing 125–129
role models 101

safety, costs of 14–16
staff 9
encouraging 104–105
role of 108–109
statistics of days lost 38–39
strategic components 26–27
structures 93
suggestion schemes 154

supervisors   105–108

targets, setting   93–94, 103–104
team, building a   167–169
training   159, 162–163, 175–182
truth, telling the   136

values and beliefs   72